J. Spencer Hill

The Indo-Chinese Opium Trade

J. Spencer Hill

The Indo-Chinese Opium Trade

ISBN/EAN: 9783744662536

Printed in Europe, USA, Canada, Australia, Japan

Cover: Foto ©Suzi / pixelio.de

More available books at **www.hansebooks.com**

THE
INDO-CHINESE OPIUM TRADE

CONSIDERED IN RELATION TO

ITS HISTORY, MORALITY, AND EXPEDIENCY,

AND

ITS INFLUENCE ON CHRISTIAN MISSIONS.

BY

J. SPENCER HILL, B.A.,

SCHOLAR OF ST. JOHN'S COLLEGE, CAMBRIDGE.

BEING THE ESSAY WHICH OBTAINED THE MAITLAND PRIZE OF THE UNIVERSITY FOR 1882.

WITH PREFATORY NOTE
BY THE RIGHT HON. LORD JUSTICE FRY.

LONDON:
HENRY FROWDE,
AMEN CORNER, PATERNOSTER ROW.
1884.

TO

MY FATHER AND MOTHER.

ADVERTISEMENT.

I SHOULD not have published this Essay, which was fortunate enough to obtain the Maitland Prize in the University of Cambridge, had it not been required by the regulations of that foundation. Some may think the treatment of the subject one-sided. I can only say that I commenced with a strong prejudice against the Anti-Opium agitators; but my investigation of the facts and arguments on both sides of the case compelled me to adopt their views, and forced me to the conclusion that our connection with the traffic is wholly unjustifiable. In such a hackneyed subject originality is necessarily impossible, and I have, of course, made the fullest use of all available information: as however so much of what has been written on this question is common property, I have not thought it needful to give references in every case, and hope that this general acknowledgment of my indebtedness will be sufficient.

J. S. H.

ST. JOHN'S COLLEGE, CAMBRIDGE,
    March, 1884.

PREFATORY NOTE

BY THE

RIGHT HON. LORD JUSTICE FRY.

THE MAITLAND PRIZE in the University of Cambridge was founded by the friends of the late Sir Peregrine Maitland, K.C.B., late Commander-in-Chief of the Forces in South India, for an English Essay on some subject connected with the propagation of the Gospel through missionary exertions in India and other parts of the heathen world. The subject selected for the year 1882 was 'The Opium Traffic between India and China viewed politically and morally, and in its bearings on the efforts of Christian missionaries.' The following essay was successful in the competition for that prize.

I have read the essay with much interest, and I trust that it may be the means of calling the attention of many persons to what I believe to be one of the greatest sins that lie at our door as a nation. I am particularly interested in observing that Mr. Hill commenced his study of the subject with 'a strong prejudice against the anti-opium agitators,' and that he was compelled by the force of reason to concur in their conclusions.

The subject is one on which great ignorance still prevails, and it is not possible to form an intelligent opinion upon it without some study. Few of those who investigate it with honest and unbiased minds can, I believe, come to any other conclusion than that we are still year by year doing a grievous wrong to China—a wrong which, I believe, will some day, and perhaps before very long, cause to our own nation trouble and sorrow.

E. F.

February 1884.

CONTENTS.

		PAGE
CHAPTER I.	THE HISTORY OF THE TRAFFIC	1
,, II.	THE MORALITY OF THE TRAFFIC	29
,, III.	THE EXPEDIENCY OF THE TRAFFIC	61
,, IV.	THE INFLUENCE OF THE TRAFFIC ON CHRISTIAN MISSIONS	86
,, V.	CONCLUSION	92

CHAPTER I.

THE HISTORY OF THE TRAFFIC.

BEFORE 1773 the cultivation of the poppy was a monopoly maintained by the civil servants of the East India Company at its Patna factory for their own personal profit, and in direct contravention of the strict orders laid down by the Company. In that year however the Company itself assumed the management and leased it to two natives for a year only. The question of the monopoly was warmly discussed by the new Council General, appointed on the recommendation of the Indian Government by the Act of 1775. Even at that early period unfavourable comments on its working and probable results were not wanting. One of the ablest members of the Council, Mr. Philip Francis, afterwards the well-known Sir Philip Francis, declared his opinion that the monopoly of opium was highly prejudicial to the trade of Bengal; and he asserted that as the land revenue beyond all doubt suffered from its production, it was misleading to reckon the revenue gained from the drug as absolute profit to the Company. The directors, while assenting to the opinion thus expressed, thought it wiser to continue the monopoly for their own benefit than to throw it open for the benefit of individuals. Thus sanctioned, it was worked for a time by selling the permission to the highest bidder. After the first contract however had expired, Mr. Hastings, contrary to the express orders of the Directors, farmed the concession first to a Mr. Mackenzie, an Englishman, and afterwards, wishing to secure a friend in the council chamber at Leadenhall Street, he gave the contract to Mr. Stephen Sullivan, the son of the then Chairman of the Company, a young gentleman who had only just arrived in India and knew nothing whatever of the business. Up to this time, though a very small trade in the drug with China had been carried on, the bulk of the manufacture was disposed of to the Dutch merchants at Batavia. In 1781 however the war with the Dutch, which had broken out, closed this market, and Mr. Hastings had to find other purchasers for his wares. He therefore, with the consent of his council, approved a scheme for chartering a vessel expressly to sell opium in various Eastern ports, and specially to develope the existing trade with China. A principal reason for this latter undertaking was no doubt to be found in the importance of obtaining if possible some new means of sending the necessary supplies to the Company's representatives in China, who had hitherto paid for their annual purchases in tea and other Chinese commodities in bullion. This method of payment however, always inconvenient, now made itself particularly felt, as the other presidencies were at this time drawing largely on Calcutta, and the advantage of making the annual payments to China in Indian produce instead of specie was of course obvious. Consequently we need not be surprised that Mr. Hastings, as already mentioned, should have entertained the proposal. It was first made by a Colonel Watson, who in a letter to the Board of Revenue, written early in 1781, suggested that the Company should endeavour to trade immediately with the North or Eastern ports of China, as it would at least act beneficially in counteracting the monopoly of the Hong merchants at Canton, who by their arbitrary and unrestrained methods of dealing seriously inconvenienced the Company's trade at that port.

Though neither Mr. Hastings nor his council appear to

have so looked at the matter, yet the proposed undertaking was really nothing else than a smuggling adventure against China openly carried out by the responsible rulers of British India. For that the edict of Kea-King in 1796 was not, as is commonly supposed, the first prohibition of opium in China can be clearly proved. In the report of the Committee of 1783, Appendix 77, we find the following letter from Mr. Fitz-Hugh to Mr. Gregory on the subject of exporting opium to China, and severely condemning the project. 'The importation of opium to China,' says Mr. Fitz-Hugh, 'is forbidden by very severe penalties. The 'opium on seizure is destroyed, the vessel in which it is 'brought to the port is confiscated, and the Chinese in 'whose possession it is found for sale is punishable with 'death.' After remarking that the trade, though thus prohibited, has been carried on by the English and Portuguese, and referring to the high estimation in which the Company are held by the Chinese, he thus concludes, 'How must this 'opinion change when your servants are on the Company's 'account to deviate from the plain road of honourable trade 'to pursue the crooked paths of smuggling.' But to return to our story. Colonel Watson did something more than merely suggest. He offered his own ship, the *Nonsuch*, to carry the opium to China, and the offer was accepted, while his requests for cannon, soldiers, and medical stores—hardly suggestive of a peaceable trading venture—were all agreed to. The terms of the arrangement—that not less than 2000 chests should be sent, for which the Board of Revenue agreed to allow 50 Sicca rupees a chest as freight from Bengal to Canton—were so advantageous that similar offers were made by other persons, and another ship was engaged to carry 1490 chests of the drug on the same errand to the Straits of Malacca and the Chinese coast.

The speculation however was not a success. The supercargoes of the Company at Canton were both surprised and perplexed by this new development of their business, and in their letters to Calcutta they say:—'The importation of 'opium being strongly prohibited by the Chinese, and a 'business altogether new to us, it was necessary to take our 'measures with the utmost caution.' They were in fact compelled to be satisfied with the very low price of 210 dollars per chest, and in writing to the Court of Directors they strongly disapproved of the new enterprise. The Court itself indeed condemned the whole transaction in the strongest terms, and in the course of their despatch on the subject the Directors say, 'with regard to the consignment of 2000 chests 'of opium immediately to the supercargoes to be disposed of 'as they shall think proper, we have been informed that the 'importation of opium into China is forbidden on very severe 'penalties. . . . Under any circumstances it is beneath the 'Company to be engaged in such a clandestine trade: we 'therefore positively prohibit any more opium being sent to 'China on the Company's account.' Unfortunately, however, the Directors, in accordance with their usual habit, contented themselves with ordering the cessation of the enterprise without taking the needful steps to enforce their commands. As Macaulay well says, their despatches contain many excellent precepts and an admirable code of political ethics, but the force of the exhortation was always nullified by a demand for money. And their attitude towards the opium trade was no exception to the general rule. In common with many other people, they desired to share the profits of evil doing without the odium and ill repute which were its necessary concomitants. Indeed, in one despatch we find them, after piously observing 'that they would on no account wish to be 'concerned with an illicit trade,' proposing the opening of communications with the Eastern ports of China. 'We 'might,' they continue, 'then meet with a market for the

'whole produce of our opium farms ... and whatever opium
'might be in demand with the Chinese, the quantity would
'readily find its way thither, without the Company being
'exposed to the disgrace of engaging in an illicit commerce.'
In 1796 however the Chinese government, distrusting one
might almost fancy such a superficial and hollow morality,
began to take alarm, and the Emperor issued a proclamation
enforcing with additional penalties the existing restrictions on
the importation of the drug. In view of the new edicts the
supercargoes at Canton strongly urged the necessity of laying
some additional restraint on the servants of the Company to
prevent them from engaging in a traffic so recently condemned
by the Chinese authorities. The Company, though quite ready
to profit by the evil doings of others, was fully alive to the
necessity of maintaining its own reputation. Accordingly,
stringent regulations were issued, which forbade any servant
of the Company on pain of immediate dismissal to carry any
contraband article to China. But though the Company thus
acknowledged itself responsible to the Chinese government
for the honourable trading of its own servants, with its usual
inconsistency it encouraged, or at least did not attempt to
prevent, the systematic violation of Chinese regulations by all
other traders. For during all this time the control of the
Company over ships trading to China was absolute. Every
captain sailing to China bound himself to obey the orders of
the Company's supercargoes at Canton, so that nothing could
have been easier than for the Company to have stopped the
trade, if there had been any real desire to do so. But the
traffic was far too lucrative, and if it was inexpedient to undertake the actual introduction of the drug to the Chinese consumer, no such reasons could be urged against manufacturing
it for those who were not hampered by such unfortunate
restrictions. Accordingly, the Company continued deliberately
and openly to grow and prepare the drug for the Chinese

market. Every seer of the drug produced was openly sold at Calcutta to the opium merchants and shipped off for 'China direct,' unhindered, and unimpeded. Nay more. On one occasion at least the Indian Government actually paid (Pros and Cons of the Opium Trade, p. 21) a large sum to those engaged in the trade, and who had suffered in consequence of a stoppage occasioned by unwonted severity and activity on the part of the Chinese authorities. The Directors indeed expressed 'their utter repugnance to the trade, and longed to 'abolish the consumption of the drug': but to ordinary minds the increased production of the 'pernicious' article appears a most extraordinary method of carrying out their benevolent intentions.

The Chinese authorities continued to expostulate, and in 1821 the Governor of Canton took active measures to suppress the traffic. The opium vessels, however, when driven from Whampoa, merely retired to Lintin, an island close to the mouth of the Canton river, where they established themselves, and the trade 'almost assumed a regular character.' The attempts made to extend operations along the coast were generally successful, and the local authorities, finding themselves unable to drive away the opium dealers, contented themselves with the easier process of issuing mere paper edicts, and connived, for a consideration, at a trade to repress which they lacked either the energy or the power.

Matters remained thus till 1834, when the termination of the Company's monopoly, and the consequent opening of the trade, commenced a new chapter in the history of the Company, and seriously modified the conditions under which the trade with China had hitherto been carried on. For not only did the new order of things abolish the select body of traders with whom alone China had hitherto had any dealings: it extended at the same time to all British traders—men who had been specially distinguished from the Company's ser-

vants, and had rendered themselves obnoxious to the Chinese government by their notorious smuggling and other irregular operations—the right to open communications with the most exclusive of nations. Nor was this all. Before the trade was thus thrown open the control exercised by the Company's supercargoes had been some guarantee for the good behaviour of British traders, but now even this slight check was removed and no new method of supervision was substituted in its stead. Moreover the action of the British Government at this conjuncture, though no doubt well-intentioned, was in effect most unfortunate. Lord Napier was appointed to the new office of Superintendent of British trade in China, and while one paragraph of his instructions enjoined him 'to avoid all such conduct, language, and de-
'meanour ... as might unnecessarily irritate the feelings or
'revolt the opinions or prejudices of the Chinese people or
'government,' it was a cardinal point of his mission to introduce direct communication with the provincial authorities, a claim which had never been conceded to the supercargoes of the Company, and was wholly contrary to established usage and precedent. When he reached the outer waters of Canton in July 1834, and his arrival had been made known in an unofficial manner to the authorities, the Hong merchants, who hitherto had been the recognised medium of communication between foreigners and the governor, were instructed to explain to him the state of the case. He declined to receive them. Thereupon, in consequence of this refusal on the part of the English to receive communications from the Chinese through the persons appointed for the purpose, the Hong merchants were required to stop the trade, and this was done on the 16th of August. In return, Lord Napier most unwisely published in Canton a statement denouncing the conduct of the governor in language which, to say the least, was most impolitic. On the 7th of September

he determined to try the effect of force, and in direct contravention of his instructions, ordered his ships of war to force their way through the entrance of the Canton river. This they succeeded in doing, in spite of the forts on the river, and took up their station under the walls of Canton. The Chinese, however, steadily held their ground, and refused to hold any communication with him or to permit any trade until the ships were withdrawn. The English merchants, at length finding that the stoppage of the trade was becoming serious, urged upon him more conciliatory measures, and in consequence of their representations, and of failing health, he yielded and, amid the taunts and insults of the Chinese, withdrew to Macao, where he died soon afterwards. Though we may well sympathise with his troubles and deplore his untimely fate, yet we cannot exonerate Lord Napier from blame in this matter. He was no doubt placed in a very difficult position, and his instructions were certainly out of harmony with the plain facts of the case. At the same time it must be pointed out that the spirit in which he executed his mission was most harsh and unconciliatory. An envoy who says, as he does in one of his despatches, 'I cannot for 'one moment suppose that in dealing with such a nation Her 'Majesty's Government will be ruled by the ordinary forms 'prescribed among civilized peoples;' who urges Her Majesty's Government to 'command' a commercial treaty, and who thinks it 'would be worthy of the greatness and the 'power of England' to 'demand the same personal privileges 'for all traders that every trader enjoys in England' on pain of 'abiding the consequences—all the horrors of a bloody 'war against a defenceless people,' was certainly not the man to negotiate successfully with a nation so sensitive and jealous as the Chinese. They may have been exclusive, supercilious, and overbearing, but the spirit of brutal greed and violence which Lord Napier sanctioned could only make reconciliation and a good understanding still more difficult, even if it did not actually pave the way for the wars and troubles which ultimately followed.

Soon after the reopening of trade the Chinese authorities, through the Hong merchants, requested the English Government to appoint a commercial superintendent of the trade without delay, thus showing that they looked at the matter merely as a question of trade, not in the international aspect in which it was so persistently regarded by Lord Palmerston and the English Government. The words of the Governor of Canton make this very clear. 'Let,' says he, 'a *commer-* '*cial man* be appointed by the said nation to become a 'superintendent, and come to China to direct and control. 'This is *a matter of buying and selling:* it is not what military 'officers can attend to the management of. In the inner 'land the Hong merchants are always held responsible, and 'so too the said nation must positively select and appoint 'a trading man. On no account should a government officer 'be again appointed to occasion, as Lord Napier did, the 'creation of trouble and disturbance.'—(China Papers, 1840, p. 55.) In other words, what the Chinese desired was the re-establishment of the purely trade supervision previously exercised by the supercargoes of the East India Company.

For some time after the death of Lord Napier his successor, Sir George Robinson, as far as possible adopted this view of his position, and established his head-quarters at Lintin for the better regulation of the general trade. In his despatches to the home government he argued strongly in favour of the course he had adopted, and urged that the duties of the superintendent should be 'to receive the registers and papers 'of ships arriving, and to issue distinct and precise orders for 'the guidance of captains, who should appeal to him in all 'serious cases of disturbance and complaint on board ship, 'and invariably where natives of China are concerned, in-

'stead of taking the law into their own hands and seeking to
'redress their real or imaginary grievances : to listen patiently
'to any Chinese who may be aggrieved, and by the power
'with which he is invested to afford them redress, and if pos-
'sible indemnification; to attend to the better ordering and
'discipline of the ships, by watchful observation over both
'commanders and seamen; and by every means in his power
'to improve and ameliorate the present disorganised state of
'the mercantile marine.'—(China Papers, 1840, p. 116.) Such
a view of his official position, incidentally disclosing as it
does a state of things hardly creditable to the character of
British traders, required for its satisfactory accomplishment
more definite powers and authority than that with which the
superintendents had been invested. Lord Palmerston however, while 'recognising the inconveniences of the existing
'state of things, and hoping that at no distant period some
'effectual remedy may be provided,' recommended him 'at
'present to confine his interference as much as possible to
'friendly suggestion and advice.'—(China Papers, 1840, p.
128.) Eventually the Government, obviously in the interests
of the opium trade, declined to adopt his proposal, and
recalled him, though the policy he followed was completely
acceptable to the Chinese and resulted in a decided increase
of trade, and appointed Captain Elliott as superintendent in
his place, with earnest instructions to establish if possible
political communication with the Chinese Government.

Meanwhile, the importance of the question had engaged
the serious attention of the highest authorities in China.
Memorials were presented to the Emperor both in favour of,
and adverse to, the policy of legalising the trade; and
though we may call the Chinese barbarians and uncivilised,
yet a perusal of the arguments urged in the different documents cannot but impress the unbiased reader with a high
sense of the acuteness and statesmanlike views which they

display. In urging its legalisation, Heu Naetze, Vice-President of the Sacrificial Court, pointed out that the existing laws had fallen into disuse, and that it was impracticable to prohibit the illicit importation of the drug, not only because of the negligence and corruption of the 'extortionate underlings,' but also because the carrying-boats plying up and down the river 'are well armed with guns and other weapons, 'and are manned with some scores of desperadoes.' The same argument was urged by the Governor of Canton in his report on the subject, and he also proposed various rules for the due regulation of the trade in the event of its legislation. On the other side, Choo Tsun, member of the Council of the Board of Rites, protested against the doctrine that laws should be allowed to fall into desuetude, maintaining that their vigorous execution was quite possible, and that their occasional abuse was no reason for their repeal. After contending that the levy of a duty is improper and ill-beseeming, and that if the exportation of sycee silver can be prevented, it was also possible to prohibit the importation of opium, he earnestly drew attention to the serious material and moral damage inflicted on the people by the use of the drug. 'In the people,' he says, 'lies the very foundation of em- 'pire. A deficiency of property may be supplied, but it is 'beyond the power of any artificial means to save a people 'enervated by luxury.' And he declares that the object of the English 'in introducing opium into this country has 'been to weaken and enfeeble the Celestial Empire.' Heu Kew, a Censor of the Military Department, supported this view, and urged the strict enforcement of the laws against the habit. Every smoker guilty of its use should be punished, and the foreign traders required to desist, or to leave the country. 'They should be required,' he proposes, 'to write 'a letter to the queen of their country, telling her that opium 'is a poison which has pervaded the inner land to the material

'injury of the people: that the Celestial Empire has in-
'flicted on all the traitorous natives who sold it the severest
'penalties: that with regard to themselves, the resident
'foreigners, the Government taking into consideration that
'they are barbarians and aliens, forbears to pass sentence of
'death upon them; but that if the opium ships will desist
'from coming to China, they shall be indulgently released
'and permitted to continue their commercial intercourse as
'usual: whereas, if they will again build receiving-vessels,
'and bring them hither to entice the natives, the commercial
'intercourse granted them in teas, silks, etc., shall assuredly
'be altogether interdicted, and on the resident foreigners of
'the said nation the laws shall be executed capitally.' 'While
'in their own country,' he goes on to say, 'no opium is
'smoked, the barbarians yet seek to poison therewith the
'people of the central flowery land. ... Of late the foreign
'vessels have presumed to make their way into every place,
'and to cruise about in the inner seas. Is it likely that in
'this they have no evil design of spying out our real strength
'or weakness?'

Before however deciding between the two views here set forth, the Emperor determined to take the opinion of the various officials throughout the Empire—a notable instance of an absolute despotism referring an all-important question to the arbitrament of those who were best calculated to form a correct judgment, and who would be most affected by the decision. Unfortunately for the contentions and the confident expectations of the opium dealers, among whom were nine-tenths of the British merchants trading to China, the great majority of the reports received were unfavourable to the traffic and urged its immediate and entire prohibition. Acting on this advice, the Chinese Emperor determined to attempt the suppression of the traffic. He despatched the well-known Commissioner Lin to Canton invested with the fullest powers

for effectually accomplishing the work, and issued the most stringent orders for the enforcement of the laws against the sale and importation of the drug. Some time before urgent representations had been addressed to Captain Elliott requesting him to send away the opium receiving-ships. In accordance with our usual policy, these requests were not complied with, but were met in a spirit of the most dishonourable evasion. The British Representative replied that he was Superintendent of the regular trade alone, and could take no cognisance of the illegitimate traffic which did not come under the terms of his commission. The rejoinder of the Chinese Governor to this piece of diplomatic shuffling is so natural, and so much to the point, that it may be inserted verbatim. 'The vessels,' observes the Governor, 'having
' been so long anchored off the coast that the great Emperor
' has been informed respecting them, and the Superintendent
'having resided for some years at Macao, how can he be
' ignorant of the circumstances and places of their anchorage?
' . . . The king of the said nation being apprehensive lest
' merchants and seamen coming hither should infringe pro-
' hibitions and transgress the laws, and so bring shame upon
' their country, he specially sent Superintendent Elliott to
' Canton to keep them under control and restraint. But
' these two receiving-ships have now remained for a very long
' time at anchor, and though two months have passed since
' the said Superintendent received our commands he has not
' yet sent them away to their country. We fear he is unfit to
' bear the designation of Superintendent. If he can willingly
' subject himself to reproach on account of these receiving-
' vessels how will he be able to answer to his king?'—(China Papers, 1840, p. 239.) To an ordinary mind the contention of the Governor is unassailable, and we who now read it can only blush to think that those who were responsible for the honour of England abroad should in the first place have deserved, and

in the second place done nothing to free themselves from, the bitter reproaches which such a document contains.

Towards the end of the year preceding the arrival of Lin at Canton the stringent measures of the Chinese, as we learn from Captain Elliott, 'had produced a complete and very ' hazardous change in the whole manner of conducting the ' trade.' In other words, as the vigilance of the Chinese had made it difficult for the opium dealers to obtain the services of native smugglers, they were now obliged to employ Europeans, who were (Fry, ' Facts and Evidences of the Opium Trade,' p. 28) generally 'a set of desperate fellows who would ' not stick at burning and destroying anything that might ' prevent them from disposing of their opium.' Under these circumstances one need not wonder at the anxiety of Captain Elliott to hide these iniquities under the decent cloak of legalisation. When however he advised that the Chinese Government should be informed ' that her Majesty was without ' the power to prevent or to regulate the traffic,' he can hardly have considered the impression which such a confession of English administrative impotence would be likely to make on the Chinese government.

Though in January, 1839, Captain Elliott reported that ' the stagnation of the trade may be said to have been nearly ' complete for the last four months,' the ten British receiving-ships still lay at Lintin with more than 20,000 chests of opium on board, hoping for a favourable opportunity to dispose of them. When therefore the Chinese Commissioner arrived at Canton on March 10, these ships first claimed his attention; and as repeated requests to the Superintendent to send them away had merely produced renewed protestations of his inability to do so, Lin was compelled to resort to forcible measures to effect the object of his mission. Accordingly, he at once issued an order to foreigners of all nations, requiring them to deliver up all the opium in their storeships. He also demanded from them a bond that for the future they would altogether abstain from attempts to introduce opium into the country. 'I have heard,' the edict continued, 'that you foreigners are used to attach great import-'ance to the words "good faith." If, then, you will really do 'as I have commanded, deliver up every particle of opium that 'is already here, and will stay its future introduction ... the 'past may be left unnoticed ... you will continue to enjoy 'the advantages of commercial intercourse, will be enabled 'to acquire profits by an honest trade, and will you not indeed 'stand in a most honourable position? If however you 'obstinately adhere to your folly, and refuse to awake: if 'you think to make up a tale covering your illicit dealings, 'and pretend that the merchants have nothing to do with it, '... it will be evident that you retain a spirit of contumacy, 'that you uphold vice and will not reform.' The cogent logic and the forcible appeal of this edict must be apparent even to those who are most prejudiced against the Chinese, and if 'gain-seeking desires had not cauterised their souls,' to use the biting words of the Governor of Canton, the opium merchants themselves must have winced at some of its passages. Three days were allowed for obedience to the edict, which was of course wholly ignored by the foreign merchants. When they had elapsed, Lin surrounded the foreign factories at Canton, and informed the inhabitants that until the opium at Lintin was given up a strict blockade would be maintained. At this juncture Captain Elliott joined them, but though he planted the English flag on the factories, he was not treated with more consideration than the others. At length, in order to free himself and his companions, he took upon himself the responsibility of ordering the merchants to give up the opium to him for delivery to the Chinese government, 'holding himself re-'sponsible in the most free and unreserved manner for and

'on behalf of Her Majesty's government to all and each of
' Her Majesty's subjects surrendering the said British-owned
' opium into his hands to be delivered over to the Chinese
' government.' His orders were quickly obeyed, for the opium merchants looked upon the transaction as a most fortunate sale of unsaleable opium to the British government; and 20,285 chests—an amount amply proving that the trade was almost wholly confined to the British subjects—were duly surrendered, the blockade was raised, and the imprisoned merchants liberated. Contrary to the confident anticipations of the opium merchants, to whom such a proceeding was inconceivable, the Emperor ordered the entire destruction of the opium—though valued at more than three million sterling—and his commands were faithfully carried out. In the words (quoted in Fry, 'Facts and Evidences,' p. 17) of an eye-witness, 'the degree of care and fidelity with which the ' work of destruction was conducted far exceeded our ex-
' pectations, and I cannot conceive how any business could
' be more faithfully executed.'

In reviewing this crucial proceeding of the Chinese Commissioner, the crowning act of his policy, and the principal cause of the war with England which immediately followed, while it cannot be admitted with Captain Elliott that 'the ' demand was an act of forcible spoliation of the very worst ' description' (Ch. Papers, 1840, p. 389), it may be acknowledged that it was hardly in accordance with the strict letter of the law. The opium ships, being stationed in the 'outer waters' of Canton, were technically beyond the jurisdiction of the Chinese government, while the rough and ready mode of imprisoning the whole of the foreign residents could only be justified by extreme necessity. At the same time, it should be remembered that legal technicalities have never maintained in similar crises the force or validity which at other times they are supposed to possess, while the connection of the whole foreign community with the prohibited traffic, and the repeated failures of the Chinese authorities to obtain the dismissal of the ships from the English Superintendent, almost warrant us in holding, with an English judge (Sir Edward Fry, 'England, China, and Opium,' p. 9), 'that the 'demand of the Chinese government appears not to have 'been unreasonable, or beyond the rights of a sovereign state 'in defence of its own institutions, and for the protection of ' 'its people from what it honestly believed to be a curse.'

The details of the war which ensued—a war concerning which public opinion has ratified the emphatic declaration of Mr. Gladstone that justice was on the side of the Pagan not the Christian—need not be here related. Of course the Chinese, though they made a gallant resistance, were utterly defeated, and compelled to accept any terms of peace which the English conquerors chose to dictate. These were embodied in the Treaty of Nankin, signed in August 1842, the main stipulations of which were the following: Five ports— Canton, Amoy, Foochow, Ningpo, and Shanghai—were to be opened to British trade, and British goods were to be admitted at a very moderate duty. The Chinese were to pay six million dollars for the destroyed opium—a stipulation hardly consonant with another clause enacting, that 'if any smuggle 'goods the goods will be liable to confiscation'—three million dollars for debts due to British subjects by the Hong merchants, and twelve million dollars as a war indemnity. Hong Kong was also to be ceded to England.[1] All these conditions were duly carried out, but as the feeling at Canton was so hostile to the English, the opening of that port was deferred for the present.

In all these transactions the attitude of England is hardly

[1] 'For the purpose of careening and refitting ships,' a clause inserted to please the Emperor who contemplated nothing more in the cession.

one which can command our admiration. It may be allowed that the arrogance and exclusiveness of the Chinese were very galling to our national pride; and the opinion of many excellent authorities, that chastisement to enforce concessions and more courteous treatment was inevitable, may be well founded. At the same time it must be remembered that these methods of dealing and communication, undignified though they were, had been readily assented to by the East India Company, and that the Chinese, with their imperfect knowledge of European affairs and their stereotyped modes of action, could hardly have been expected to change them hastily, or to admit the favourite contention of Lord Palmerston as to the indefeasible rights of a British subject. And further, it is at least a disputed question how far one state is justified in forcing another to enter into communication with it. In private life the theory is, as we all know, entirely rejected, and in international relations is at least not gaining ground. Still, even if both these considerations be decided against the Chinese, our obvious patronage of, or at least our failure to prevent our own subjects from engaging in, the illicit traffic in opium, which was certainly the primary cause of the war, must count heavily in our disfavour. How much better, how much more 'worthy of the power and greatness of England,
' would it have been had we used that power to put down the
' opium traffic, as far as we were concerned, by suppressing
' the cultivation of the drug in India, and preventing, as far as
' possible, British subjects from selling it in the China seas.
' Would not such a course have commanded the respect and
' gratitude both of the government and of the people of
' China?' Would it not have 'been lovely and of good report
' among the nations of the earth' if we had cleared ourselves from all participation in the unholy commerce, and had assisted, instead of hindering, the Chinese government in its honest endeavours to suppress what it at least believed to be

a stupendous evil. Unhappily for our fair fame and for the future of China the opportunity was missed, and no attempt was made to deserve a more favourable estimation among the Chinese than our shot and shell were able to procure for us. But, cowed and defeated as the Chinese were, they altogether refused to sanction the legalisation of opium, and though this permission was an important point in his instructions, the English representative was quite unable to obtain it. When however the subject was raised in private conversation, the Chinese Commissioner Keying anxiously asked why the British would not assist the Chinese to suppress the trade? The English negotiator replied that the development of the trade was chiefly due to the corruption of the Chinese officials, and to the inability of the Chinese government either to suppress smuggling or to enforce their own edicts among their own people: and that if the British did not satisfy the craving of the Chinese people for the drug, other nations would. Afterwards, in writing to the governor of Hong Kong, Keying, the Chinese Commissioner, in reply to his proposals for the legalisation of the drug, says (Ch. Papers, 1842–1856, p. 21): 'It would indeed be to the advantage ' of the Chinese revenues if, as you observe, opium paid ' duties like all legal articles, whereby smuggling would like- ' wise be avoided. But whilst looking to benefit the customs, ' and allowing foolish and ignorant people to use this article ' so injurious to man, we should thus certainly put a value on ' riches and slight men's lives.' But though the Chinese thus steadily refused to legalise the trade, and fully retained the right of confiscating it as contraband, they hardly dared to exercise their power. The action of the British had made it perfectly plain that they were at least not unfavourable to the trade, and after their late experience the Chinese naturally concluded that any interference with the opium smugglers would only involve them in new difficulties with the British nation. The edicts against opium therefore were no longer issued, and the laws against it, though not repealed, were seldom or never enforced. Under these circumstances we need not wonder that the traffic more than recovered from its momentary stagnation, and indeed grew apace. The opium ships cruised up and down the coast, while the receiving vessels anchored comfortably and openly in the near neighbourhood of the treaty ports. Piracy and smuggling, fostered by European intervention, surpassed all previous limits, and to the scum of Oriental populations who had always infested the Chinese waters were now added the refuse of the European peoples. At Hong Kong, now made a free port, the basest and most lawless of the Chinese congregated in great numbers. Free from their own police, and under a lax and careless administration, they obtained facilities for their illegal trading which enabled them safely to defy any preventive service which the Chinese government might employ. By an arrangement, which now seems hardly credible though it was a notorious fact, a colonial register, carrying with it liberty to use the English flag and all its unequalled privileges, was granted to any Chinese who resided in the colony. As Sir John Bowring, the Governor of Hong Kong, expressed it (Corresp. concerning Colonial Registers at Hong Kong), 'a vessel no sooner obtains a register 'than she escapes colonial jurisdiction, carries on her trade 'within the waters of China, engages probably in every sort of 'fraudulent dealing, and may never again appear to render any 'account of her proceedings or to be made responsible for 'her illegal acts.' How a state of things so flagrantly dishonourable and so openly disgraceful to the British flag can not only have been tolerated but actually encouraged is almost unaccountable. Such a manifest abuse could hardly fail to make our name stink in the nostrils of the people and to cause sooner or later the rupture between the two nations, of which the boarding of the lorcha 'Arrow' by command of Commissioner Yeh in the Canton river on October 8th, 1856, was the immediate occasion. The stubborn contention of Yeh that the vessel was Chinese and not British, a contention of sufficient strength to obtain the assent of an English Chancellor, and the indecent haste with which Sir John Bowring, inspired by his 'monomania' of entering Canton, pressed on hostilities, are too well known to need recapitulation. Nor need we linger over the incidents of the war, or that supreme act of Vandalism, the burning of the Emperor's Summer Palace at Pekin, further than to point out the result of this force and violence on 'the obstinate morality' of the Chinese government. For our purpose the interest of the whole scene centres in the supplementary agreement to the treaty of Tientsin, which was concluded at Shanghai on the 8th of November, 1858, and in particular on the fifth Article of that agreement. It is headed, ' Regarding certain commodities 'heretofore contraband,' and is in the following terms :—' The 'restrictions affecting trade in opium, cash, grain, pulse, 'sulphur, brimstone, saltpetre, and spelter, are relaxed under 'the following conditions :—Opium will henceforth pay 30 'taels per picul import duty. The importer will sell it only at 'the port. It will be carried into the interior by Chinese only, 'and only as Chinese property; the foreign trader will not be 'allowed to accompany it. The provision of Article 9 of the 'Treaty of Tientsin, by which British subjects are authorised 'to proceed into the interior with passports to trade, will not 'extend to it ; nor will those of Article 28 of the same Treaty, 'by which the transit dues are regulated ; the transit dues on 'it will be arranged as the Chinese Government see fit ; nor 'in future revisions of the tariff is the same rule of revision to 'be applied to opium as to other goods.' In the history of our relations with China this clause is of the highest importance, as it was the first occasion in which the Chinese Government legalised the trade in opium. While it is perfectly 'true that 'Lord Elgin postponed the subject till the Supplementary 'Treaty, because he could not reconcile it to his sense of right 'to urge the Chinese Government to abandon its traditional 'policy under the kind of pressure which he brought to bear 'upon it at Tientsin;' and while it may also be perfectly true that Messrs. Lay and Oliphant are correct in asserting (as they are quoted in the recent despatch of the Indian Government), that 'the Chinese Government admitted opium as a legal 'article of import not under constraint, but of their free will 'deliberately,' it can hardly be doubted that the pressure which operated on the Imperial Government at Tientsin in June, 1858, was also operating on them at Shanghai on the 8th of November in the same year. Lord Elgin tells us (quoted in the *Nonconformist* for Nov. 11, 1880), that the Chinese and English Commissioners met at Shanghai to discuss the different questions to be dealt with. One of these was the legalisation of opium under duties. When it was discussed, one of the Chinese Commissioners who had been judge at Canton, 'admitted the necessity of a change. 'China,' he said, 'still retains her objections to the use of 'the drug on moral grounds, but the present generation of 'smokers at all events must and will have opium. To deter 'the uninitiated from becoming smokers the Chinese would 'propose a very high duty, but as opposition was naturally '(mark that!) to be expected from us (i.e. the British 'Deputies), in that case it should be made as moderate as 'possible.' Further proof of the unwillingness and reluctance with which 'of their own free will deliberately' they admitted the hated drug may be found in the strange and unfriendly restrictions with which the concession was surrounded. Again, at the decennial revision of the tariff, as provided by the Treaty, the earnestness with which they urged Sir Rutherford Alcock to annul the stipulations respecting opium, form a strange and significant commentary on the 'free will' and deliberation with which they are supposed to have admitted it ten years before. Or, if this be denied, the only other alternative must be that the ten years experience of the new system had not increased the favour with which it was then regarded. After repeated appeals to the British Minister, Prince Kung, the head of the Chinese Foreign Office, presented his views in a statement of such force, acuteness, and interest, that its quotation in full, as it appears among Sir Rutherford's Evidence before the East Indian Finance Committee in 1871, may perhaps be excused. It runs as follows :—

'From Tsungli Yamen to Sir R. Alcock, July, 1869. The
' writers have on several occasions, when conversing with
' his Excellency the British Minister, referred to the opium
' trade as being prejudicial to the general interests of com-
' merce. The object of the treaties between our respective
' countries was to secure perpetual peace, but if effective
' steps cannot be taken to remove an accumulating sense of
' injury from the minds of men, it is to be feared that no
' policy can obviate sources of future trouble. Day and
' night the writers are considering this question with a view
' to its solution, and the more they reflect upon it the
' greater does their anxiety become; and hereon they cannot
' avoid addressing his Excellency very earnestly on the
' subject. That opium is like a deadly poison, that it is
' most injurious to mankind, and a most serious provocative
' of ill-feeling, is, the writers think, perfectly well-known to
' his Excellency, and it is therefore needless for them to
' enlarge further on these points. The prince [the Prince of
' Kung is the President of the Board] and his colleagues are
' quite aware that the opium trade has long been condemned
' by England as a nation, and that the right-minded merchant
' scorns to have to do with it. But the officials and people
' of this Empire, who cannot be so completely informed on

'the subject, all say that England trades in opium because
'she desires to work China's ruin, for (say they) if the
'friendly feelings of England are genuine, since it is open to
'her to produce and trade in everything else, would she still
'insist on spreading the poison of this hurtful thing through
'the Empire? There are those who say, Stop the trade by
'enforcing a vigorous prohibition against the use of the drug.
'China has the right to do so, doubtless, and might be able
'to effect it, but a strict enforcement of the prohibition
'would necessitate the taking of many lives. Now, although
'the criminals' punishment would be of their own seeking,
'bystanders would not fail to say that it was the foreign
'merchants who reduced them to their ruin by bringing the
'drug, and it would be hard to prevent general and deep-
'seated indignation; such a course would indeed tend to
'arouse popular anger against the foreigner. There are
'others again who suggest the removal of the prohibitions
'against the cultivation of the poppy. They argue that as
'there is no means of stopping the foreign (opium) trade,
'there can be no harm as a temporary measure in with-
'drawing the prohibition on its growth. We should thus
'not only deprive the foreign merchant of the main source
'of his profits, but should increase our revenue to boot.
'The sovereign rights of China are indeed competent to
'this. Such a course would be practicable, and indeed
'the writers cannot say that as a last resource it will not
'come to this: but they are most unwilling that such pro-
'hibition should be removed, holding as they do that a right
'system of government should appreciate the beneficence of
'heaven, and (seek to) remove any grievances which afflict its
'people, while to allow them to go on to destruction, though
'an increase of revenue may result, will provoke the judg-
'ment of heaven and the condemnation of men. Neither
'of the above plans indeed is satisfactory. If it be desired

'to remove the very root, and to stop the evil at its source,
' nothing will be effective but a prohibition to be enforced
' alike by both parties. Again, the Chinese merchant sup-
' plies your country with his goodly tea and silk, conferring
' thereby a benefit upon her, but the English merchant em-
' poisons China with pestilent opium. Such conduct is un-
' righteous. Who can justify it? What wonder if officials
' and people say that England is wilfully working out
' China's ruin, and has no real friendly feeling for her?
' The wealth and generosity of England is spoken of by all.
' She is anxious to prevent and anticipate all injury to her
' commercial interest. How is it then she can hesitate to
' remove an acknowledged evil? Indeed, it cannot be that
' England still holds to this evil business because she would
' lose a little revenue were she to forfeit the cultivation of
' the poppy! The writers hope that his Excellency will
' memorialise his Government to give orders in India, and
' elsewhere, to substitute the cultivation of cereals or cotton.
' Were both nations rigorously to prohibit the growth of the
' poppy, both the traffic in, and the consumption of, opium
' might be put an end to. To do away with so great an evil
' would be a great virtue on England's part. She would
' strengthen friendly relations and make herself illustrious.
' How delightful to have so great an act transmitted to after
' ages! This matter is injurious to commercial interests in
' no ordinary degree. If his Excellency the British Minister
' cannot, before it is too late, arrange a plan for a joint pro-
' hibition (of the traffic), then, no matter with what earnest-
' ness the writers may plead, they may be unable to cause
' the people to put aside all ill-feeling, and so strengthen
' friendly relations as to place them for ever beyond fear of
' disturbance. Day and night, therefore, the writers give to
' this matter most earnest thought, and overpowering is the
' distress it occasions them. Having thus presumed to

'unbosom themselves, they would feel honoured by his 'Excellency's reply.'

Though naturally no satisfactory reply could be sent by England to this appeal, yet Sir Rutherford Alcock was so impressed with the sincerity of the views it expressed that he visited Calcutta to consult the Governor-General and his Council on the matter. In answer to their enquiries he stated (Papers relating to the Opium Question, Appendix 4, Addendum) that 'He had no doubt that the abhorrence 'expressed by the Government and people of China for opium 'was genuine and deep-seated, and that he was quite con-'vinced that the Chinese government could, if it pleased, 'carry out its threat of developing cultivation to any extent. 'On the other hand, he believed that so strong was the popular 'feeling on the subject, that if Great Britain would give up 'the opium revenue, and suppress the cultivation in India, 'the Chinese government would have no difficulty in sup-'pressing it in China except in the province of Yunnan, 'where its authority is in abeyance.'

In 1869 Sir Rutherford negotiated a Commercial Convention dealing, among other subjects, with the 'Likin' tax and with opium. The Chinese proposed to raise the duty on the latter from thirty to fifty taels per chest. The opium merchants in China however took alarm at the prospect of losing their gains, which was threatened by the increased duty, and accordingly they urgently requested the Liberal government of the day to refuse the ratification. This course Lord Granville, 'though not free from doubt,' unfortunately decided to adopt. The Convention accordingly fell through, and the points it arranged remained unsettled. To these were presently added other difficulties, the long-standing question of etiquette and the murder of Mr. Margary in Yunnan. To settle these questions Sir Thomas Wade, Sir Rutherford's successor, and our late representative at Pekin, arranged what is known as the Chefoo Convention, which was signed on the 13th of September, 1876. Its main provisions were three in number. First, the settlement of the Yunnan affair; secondly, concessions by the Chinese in the matter of official intercourse; thirdly, commercial facilities by the opening of four new ports to British trade and British consuls. In return, a disputed question about the area of exemption from the 'Likin' tax was to be settled, and in the matter of opium a special arrangement was made by which it was to be deposited in bonded warehouses, liable both to a tariff duty and to the 'Likin' of the port to be collected by the customs, while the provincial governments were left free to decide the amount of 'Likin' to be collected upon its transit through their jurisdictions. Though by the Treaty of Tientsin the Chinese are at liberty to place any amount of duty on the internal transit of opium, their power to levy very high duties was really limited by the danger of smuggling between the place of import and the place of taxation. Inasmuch as the central authority in China is far from strong, while long years of irregular trading has brought smuggling almost to perfection, the limit thus imposed on the government is considerable. But if the place of import and the place of taxation be the same, the chances of smuggling are largely diminished, and the practical power of taxation much increased. In fact, as Lord Salisbury with cynical frankness put it in the House of Lords, the arrangement enables the Chinese to prevent smuggling, and thus they would have been able to raise their own internal duties on opium. 'That,' to use his own words, 'would be a result which practically would neutralize the 'policy which has hitherto been pursued by this country with 'regard to that drug,' for, according to the Shanghai General Chamber of Commerce, 'the Chinese will have it in their 'power to extinguish the India trade by the imposition of 'heavy duties.' Happily, however, any further discussion of the long delay and inaction of our Government in this matter is now unnecessary. The recent despatch of the Indian Government, on the whole question of the relations of the opium trade to the Government of India, expressly states that no further objection on the part of the Indian Government will be made to the ratification, and we may hope that the matter will at last be set right, and England released from the undignified and compromising position in which she has been placed since the Convention was negotiated.[1] We may now, perhaps, anticipate the time when our nation will walk still further in the path of righteousness, and mete out to the Chinese that full justice for which she has been waiting so long, and which she has not yet received at our hands. Should this expectation be fulfilled, there will be some reason to hope that the pages of the future, in which our intercourse with this great people shall be written, will be less disfigured by the dark records of wrong, injustice, and oppression, than the history of our past dealings with the Chinese nation.

[1] It should be said that the Chinese immediately fulfilled all their obligations under the Convention.

CHAPTER II.

THE MORALITY OF THE TRAFFIC.

THE history of the trade in Opium as set forth in the preceding pages shows that previously to the Treaty of Tientsin it was carried on mainly by British subjects with the support and protection of their government, in open defiance of the rulers of China and in direct contravention of the laws of that empire. Further, some reasons have been produced for believing that the legalisation of the traffic in 1860 was obtained from the Chinese by the exercise of force, against the conscience of the nation and the moral convictions of its most educated men, who were then, and still remain, hostile to the traffic, and sincere in their wish, though without the power, to suppress it. If the above facts are correct, it must needs be a matter of extreme difficulty, if not of absolute impossibility, to discover a standard of abstract morality by which the action of the British traders and the British Government can be justified. For the traffic must be condemned by the believer in Christian morality, the cardinal principles of which teach him to do unto others as he would have others do unto him, and offers him as his highest attainable ideal the promotion of the glory of God, the realisation of God among men. It can find no favour with the adherents of Utilitarian ethics, who hold that the greatest happiness of their fellow-men is the primary object of life, and who can find in its results to India and England no counterpoise to the misery it inflicts on the countless populations of China. Those also must denounce it and fear its disastrous consequences who, with Mr. Herbert Spencer, recognise the absolute right of each man to full freedom of action, provided always that it does not infringe the similar freedom of other men: and who, believing that nature invariably exacts a stern retribution for the violation of her eternal laws, see in each great catastrophe of history only the consequence of human wrong-doing.

If then the traffic in opium be liable to such condemnation, what can be said of the morality of the English Government which has throughout carefully fostered and supported it, and has by its superior force virtually compelled the Chinese Government to give it, however reluctantly, the imprimatur of legalisation? Politicians of both parties in the state, those who hold as their creed of political action the law of liberty laid down by Mr. Mill, equally with those who accept the law of compulsion propounded by Sir Fitz-James Stephen, can find no warrant in those principles for their action throughout the whole of this melancholy history. For it manifestly conflicts with the 'simple principle' which Mr. Mill enforces with so much eloquence, while it as obviously lacks the essential condition on which alone Sir Fitz-James Stephen rests his advocacy of compulsion. Did we live in an age or in a country where definite principles were acknowledged and followed wherever they might lead, this Essay might be content with having pointed out the fatal inconsistency between principles and practice involved in the continued permission of this trade. Unfortunately, however, we English pride ourselves on being a practical people, and are content to relegate 'abstract principles' which involve 'inconveniences' to the planet Jupiter and other less heavenly places. We are always ready to extenuate our short-comings by urging that our standard of morality should be adapted to the state of our civilisation, and that all considerations of abstract morality, such as have been referred to above, imply a higher condition of society than we have yet attained : and that, although we may perhaps reach it at the millennium, yet it is but fair that those who live in this nineteenth century should be satisfied with a somewhat lower and more immediately attainable degree of perfection.

But apart from such considerations it is not impossible that, while our failure to comply with the dictates of morality will be admitted, extenuating circumstances may be urged in the hope of qualifying the rigid verdict of guilty by some recommendation to mercy. If this be so, it is necessary to inquire what these alleged circumstances may be, and to ascertain the degree of weight which may be allowed to each of them. It appears then that practically they are the following :—That, to use the words (quoted by Moule ' The ' Opium Question,' p. 43) of Messrs. Jardine, Matheson and Company, the great opium merchants, ' the use of opium is ' not a curse but a comfort to the hard-working Chinese; that ' to many scores of thousands it has been productive of ' healthful sustentation and enjoyment.' Secondly, that the Chinese people and the Chinese Government are not sincere in their public declarations of the evils of opium : that the continued ' oozing out of sycee silver' (Lindsay, ' Is the War ' in China a just one ? ' p. 29) was the real reason of their hostility, and ' that public morality was only used as a mere ' stalking-horse ' for less ingenuous considerations. Thirdly, that the immense revenue annually accruing to the Indian exchequer from the profits of the opium monopoly ' has been ' dispensed in keeping the peace of that vast country, in ' developing its resources, improving its intercourse, ad- ' ministering pure and careful justice, introducing reforms, ' and educating the youthful population,' and that it produces these ample results without costing the Hindoos even the collection of a tax. To the considerations already adduced may perhaps be added another, that if India did not supply, and Englishmen did not carry, opium to China, either other nations would do so, or she would grow it herself, and that 'if' (to quote the last despatch from the Indian Government, pp. 13, 14) 'the cultivation of the poppy in India was alto-'gether suppressed, the result would indeed be that a con-'nexion, which is by some regarded as involving a moral 'stigma, would be terminated, but the cessation of opium 'smoking in China would be as far off as ever. India would 'suffer but China would not gain.' Such then are the principal pleas urged in extenuation of the trade. Urged as they are with weight and authority they deserve candid consideration, and should they be well founded they will go far to mitigate the condemnation which otherwise awaits our conduct.

In order then, first, to deal with the arguments urged by Messrs. Jardine, Matheson and Co., it is necessary to inquire into the real character of opium and its effects upon those who use it.

Opium is the concrete juice of the poppy and has been known from ancient times as a powerful narcotic. It is obtained by making incisions in the green capsules of the plant when nearly at maturity, from which it exudes as a milky juice that thickens in the heat of the sun into a brownish mass. This is scraped off the capsules and transferred to a little pot or 'chatty' carried under the arm. When this is filled the contents are shifted to a shallow brass dish which is kept for some time in a vertical position that the vegetable moisture may drain away. These dishes must be stirred every day that the opium may be dried equally, which will usually take three or four weeks. The opium is then placed in little earthen jars and taken to the government 'go down,' where it is tested, weighed, and credited to the grower. The drug is then put in large quantities into huge vats and mixed together according to variety and value; and by a delicate process it is manufactured into the 'golis' or balls known in commerce. This part of the operation is carefully watched by government overseers to ensure its quality being the same as that implied by the government mark. When the drug thus prepared reaches the Chinese consumer it is not fit for smoking, but has to pass through several additional processes before it is ready for the pipe. This usually consists of a tube of heavy wood fitted at the head with a cup which serves to collect the residuum or ashes which are left after combustion. The opium smoker always lies down, and reclining on his couch he holds his pipe, aptly termed by the Chinese 'yen tsiang,' i. e. the smoking pistol, so near the lamp that the bowl can be brought up to it without his moving himself. A little opium about the size of a pea is put into the hole of the pipe and set on fire at the lamp, and the fume is inhaled at one whiff that none of it may be lost. When the pipe has burned out the smoker repeats the dose until he has used all his purchase or taken his prescribed quantity. At the commencement of the smoking the smoker becomes loquacious, breaking out into boisterous and silly merriment, but this gradually yields to a vacant paleness and a shrinking of the features as the quantity increases and the narcotic acts. A deep sleep supervenes of from half an hour to three or four hours' duration, during which the pulse becomes slower, softer, and smaller than before the debauch. This sleep however is not refreshing, but a universal sinking of the mental and bodily powers is experienced, and an active desire for more is speedily created. Temperate smokers endeavour to keep within bounds, and some who have strong constitutions and still stronger resolutions continue the use of the drug within these limits for many years without disastrous effects upon their health and spirits. But in the large majority of cases moderation is impossible, as there is perhaps no form of intemperance more seducing, and in most instances the system when habituated to the drug demands a constantly increasing dose.

Such being the nature of the drug, we have now to enquire whether it is as Messrs. Jardine, Matheson and Co. allege, 'abundantly clear that the use of opium is not a 'curse, but a comfort, and a benefit to the hard-working 'Chinese, and that to many scores of thousands it has been 'productive of healthful sustentation and enjoyment.' As the decision of this point, the alleged innocuousness of the drug, is perhaps the most important in its practical bearing on the question, it will be desirable to examine it with some minuteness, and to investigate carefully the testimony which can be adduced for and against the view above stated. The only Chinese witness that can be found on this side of the question is Heu Naetze, President of the Sacrificial Court, and formerly Salt Commissioner and Judge at Canton, who, in his Memorial to the Emperor in favour of the legalisation of the opium trade about 1837 (Ch. Papers, 1840, pp. 156 seqq.), reminded his master that there are many harmless luxuries which are deadly in the excess, but that because of that excess it would be wrong to deprive the temperate of their enjoyment, and therefore, he argues, legalise the opium trade. Yet even he denounces opium smoking as a bad practice: 'a path leading to the utter waste of time and 'destruction of property:' so that Messrs. Jardine and Co. can hardly be said to have very much Chinese opinion in their favour. The next witness however is much more emphatic in their support. Sir Henry Pottinger, the English representative in the negotiations for the treaty of Nankin, after leaving China, wrote thus to the Chamber of Com-

merce at Bombay :—' I now unhesitatingly declare that after
' the most unbiased and careful observation, I have become
' convinced during my stay in China that the alleged de-
' moralising and debasing effects of opium have been and are
' vastly exaggerated. It appears to me to be unattended
' with a hundredth part of the debasement and misery which
' may be seen in our native country from the lamentable use
' of ardent spirits ;' an opinion which he restates in similar
terms in a despatch to the home Government (in Opium
Papers, 1842-66, pp. 7, 8). Mr. Consul Gardner, writing
from Chefoo in his trade report for the year 1878, also bears
similar testimony, stating, ' That many individuals suffer in
' health from excess is incontrovertible ... on the other hand,
' it is equally incontrovertible that thousands of hard-working
' people are indebted to opium smoking for the continuance
' of lives agreeable to themselves and useful to society.' Mr.
Scott, acting Consul at Kiung Chow, in his trade report for
the same year says :—' No one can strictly maintain that a
' mild indulgence results in physical or mental debility. A
' pipe of opium is to the Chinese workman what a glass of
' beer is to the English labourer, a climatic necessity.' Mr.
C. A. Winchester, formerly Consul at Shanghai, in his
evidence before the East India Finance Committee in 1871,
said :—' I may say that being a medical man I was led to
' the conclusion that there was a certain aptitude in the
' stimulant to the circumstances of the Chinese. They
' suffer greatly from febrile diseases, from diarrhœa and dys-
' entery, and in many cases, I presume that originally the
' habit of opium smoking was adopted in order to alleviate
' the annoyances and physical pain attaching to that class of
' diseases.' The strength of this testimony, which in any
case is not great, is much weakened when he goes on to
say, not only ' that there is no doubt that opium as a stimu-
' lant is attended by many evils,' but actually that he ' would

'not recommend a man to smoke opium under any circum-
'stances.' Passing now to medical witnesses, we find Dr. W.
W. Myers, of Tallow, stating (in the Report of the China
Imperial Maritime Customs for 1880–81, pp. 60 seqq.):—
'Here, in Formosa, there is a class of men, including the
'coolies, chairbearers, and couriers, who daily do an amount
'of work that is remarkable in its extent. These have for
'years been in the habit of taking a certain quantity of opium
'during the day, seldom or never varying it: and they assert
'that by so doing they at least attain a greater degree of
'comfort in carrying on their labours: and, with very few
'exceptions, I must admit that I have failed to obtain evi-
'dence which would justify me in attributing any marked
'harm to their habit.... I do most conscientiously state
'that, though I have met with instances in which the effects
'have been most marked and deplorable, still when con-
'sidered in numerical relation to the numbers who smoke
'opium I have been struck with their paucity, and my pre-
'conceived prejudices with reference to the universally bane-
'ful effects of the drug have been severely skaken.' Dr.
Ayres, Colonial Surgeon at Hong Kong, the head-quarters of
the Opium Trade, states:—'My experience of it [opium
'smoking] is that it may become a habit, but that the habit is
'not necessarily an increasing one: nine out of twelve men
'smoke a certain number of pipes a day, just as a tobacco
'smoker would, or as a wine or beer drinker might drink his
'two or three glasses a day without desiring more.... I do
'not wish to defend the practice of opium smoking, but in
'the face of recent opinions and exaggerated statements in
'respect to this vice, it is only right to record that no China
'resident believes in the terrible frequency of the dull, sodden-
'witted, debilitated opium smoker met with in print.'

The evidence of Dr. Eatwell, Opium Examiner in the
Bengal Service, is to the same effect:—'As regards the effects

'of the habitual use of the drug on the *mass* of the people,
' I must affirm that no injurious results are visible. The
'people generally are a muscular and well-formed race, the
'labouring population being capable of great exertion under a
'fierce sun, in an unhealthy climate.'

To these may be added two recent opinions which have attracted some notice. Deputy-Surgeon-General Moore, of the Indian Medical Service, has lately published in a small volume the substance of some papers on the opium question, contributed by him to an Indian Medical Journal. His views were thus summarised by the *Lancet* of April 8, 1881 :—
'He regards the use of opium in China and other countries
' as very comparable to the use of alcohol in this country.
'... The Chinese take it, almost need it, he argues, on ac-
' count of their poverty. It reduces waste of tissue, and
' it gives a more pleasant aspect to a life of monotony and
' poverty. In excess it is undoubtedly injurious, but it is
' not more so than alcohol taken in excess, and when not
' taken in excess is not injurious.' The other authority, Sir George Birdwood, M.D., 'late Professor of Materia Medica
' and Curator of the Government Central Economic Museum,
' Bombay,' in a lengthy letter to the *Times* of Dec. 6, 1881, argues strongly in favour of 'the downright innocency of
' opium-smoking... and that we are as free to introduce opium
' into China, and to raise a revenue from it in India, as to
' export our cotton, iron, or woollen manufactures into
' France:' he also affirms, that the smoking of opium cannot be otherwise than harmless, as the active principles of opium are non-volatisable, i.e. non-smokeable. This latter part of his contention he has been compelled to surrender as untenable, and contrary to the scientific facts of the case, and his opinion is therefore deprived of one of its chief claims to respect and attention.

To these testimonies may be added that of Mr. Fortune,

the well-known Chinese traveller, who 'has no hesitation in 'saying, that the number of persons who use it has been very 'much exaggerated;' and also that of Mr. Colborne Baker (quoted in the Appendix C. of the recently published despatch of the Indian Government), who says that 'in Szechuen he 'has never seen a case of opium intoxication; and that in 'that province, where opium cultivation has increased far 'beyond the proportion met with in other provinces, we find, 'in flat contradiction to what we should have expected, that 'indulgence in the drug has inflicted less injury here than 'elsewhere.' Finally, the evidence here collected, which is nearly all that can be found to corroborate the contention of Messrs. Jardine, Matheson and Co., may be wound up by the opinion of a writer in the *Chinese Repository* of December 10, 1836, who maintains that 'opium is a useful 'soother, a harmless luxury, and a precious medicine, except 'to those who abuse it. Many millions of the Chinese par-'ticipate in opium, using it as a rational and sociable article 'of luxury and hospitality.' In a second letter, replying to his opponents, he goes on further, and 'avers that opium 'taken in moderation is a healthful and exhilarating luxury.'

Such then is the testimony, it is believed nearly the whole testimony, that can be brought to substantiate the statement in question. Though seldom given without qualifications which often weaken its force, and not always by wholly unbiased deponents, still it presents a fairly strong *prima facie* case for argument which cannot be ignored. Taking it moreover in connection with the fact that China, notwithstanding the alleged injury done to her people through the drug, manifests much recuperative power and shows but few signs of decrepitude, those who maintain the contrary view, that opium is a curse to China, and injurious to her people, will have on their part to produce cogent arguments and weighty evidence if they wish their contention to prevail.

ITS MORALITY.

In the first place, however, they would point out as a significant fact the <u>almost entire absence</u> of Chinese witnesses from the case of the opium apologists. For they would urge that in a matter of this kind the opinion of those who consume the drug is of the highest importance. And this argument they would strengthen by producing on their own side an almost unanimous body of Chinese evidence. Shortly before the arrival of Lin at Canton in 1839, the governor of the province, in an address to the foreign traders with reference to the traffic in opium, asks, 'what feud have 'the people of this country with you that you should be 'willing to do them a mortal injury? . . . The Emperor's 'Special Commissioner may hourly be looked for. His 'purpose is to cut off utterly the source of this noxious 'abuse, to strip bare and root up this enormous evil.' In a conversation with Sir Rutherford Alcock at Pekin in May 1869, Wen-Seang, 'by far the most important man in 'the government,' admitting that there might be some of the *literati* imbued with a hostile feeling towards the foreigners, asked, how could it be otherwise? 'They had often seen 'foreigners making war upon the country: and then, again, 'how irreparable and continuous was the injury (not the 'benefit) which they saw inflicted upon the whole empire by 'the foreign importation of opium. . . . No doubt there was 'a very strong feeling entertained by all the *literati* and 'gentry as to the frightful evils attending the smoking of 'opium, its thoroughly demoralising effects, and the utter 'ruin brought upon all who once give way to the vice. 'They believed the extension of this pernicious habit was 'mainly due to the alacrity with which foreigners supplied 'the poison for their own profit, frequently regardless of the 'irreparable injury inflicted, and naturally they felt hostile to 'all concerned in the traffic.'

The opinion expressed by the Chinese Foreign Board, in

the Memorial to Sir Rutherford Alcock, is to the same effect, but having already been quoted it need not be again transcribed. To these official Chinese testimonies may be added that of a Chinese then resident in London (as given in the *Times* of July 6, 1875), and the interest of the evidence may, it is hoped, excuse the length of the quotation: 'I have not,' he says, 'the least hesitation in at once recording my firm 'belief that so far from being harmless, it [opium] is poison-'ous. This is not my individual belief, for all my country-'men, whether opium smokers or not, believe it to be so, and 'call it by that name. . . . As a Chinese I can testify to the 'innumerable instances in which my poor countrymen have 'been entirely ruined through the use of the poisonous drug. '. . . It has however been urged with some plausibility that 'opium may be, and is, used in moderate quantities without 'any ill effects ensuing. . . . Now, being a Chinese, from my 'experience and personal observation gained by my coming 'in contact daily with a large number of my friends and 'relatives, who, I am sorry to say, are opium smokers, I 'am enabled to say that such a conclusion is wrong . . . . 'even the opium smokers admit that the use of opium, except 'for medicinal purposes, is invariably more or less injurious, 'according to the physical constitution of the smoker. . . . 'Show me one instance where a man had been adhering to 'a fixed allowance of opium with which he had commenced 'four years ago, and I will show you a hundred cases where 'men began with a very moderate quantity but within ten years 'they increased their allowance to such an extent that they 'were ruined. I hope I have said enough to show the evil 'effects of opium, which every sensible man deplores. I 'would not have dwelt so much upon a topic apparently so 'clear had not an attempt been made in some quarters to 'prove the contrary.'

After making every deduction for Chinese insincerity, and

for the semi-barbarous love of exaggeration which may perhaps be charged against them, it may be submitted that the evidence from them first tendered, both private and official, points rather to the refutation than to the support of the views on opium propounded by the opium merchants; and even, if this be disputed, that it is at any rate more emphatic and influential than the solitary Chinese testimony that can be produced on the other side.

But let us turn now from Chinese to English opinion. The Directors of the East India Company early in the history of the traffic wrote to the Governor in Council in Bengal as follows (Rep. 1831, on the affairs of the East Ind. Co., App. p. 11):—' We wish it at the same time to be 'clearly understood that our sanction is given to these mea-'sures [for supplying a quantity of opium for the internal 'consumption of the country] not with a view to the revenue 'which they may yield, but in the hope that they will tend to 'restrain the use of this pernicious drug, and that the regu-'lations for the internal sale will be so framed as to prevent 'its introduction into districts where it is not used, and to 'limit its consumption in other places as nearly as possible 'to what may be absolutely necessary. Were it possible to 'prevent the use of the drug altogether we would gladly do ' 'so in compassion to mankind.' To much the same effect Mr. St. George Tucker, an eminent Indian merchant and Chairman of the Directors, is quoted by Mr. Medhurst (Parl. Papers, 1856, p. 82) as saying,—'If a revenue cannot be 'drawn from such an article otherwise than by quadrupling 'the supply . . . no fiscal considerations can justify our in-'flicting on the Malays and Chinese so grievous an evil.'

The testimony of Mr. C. A. Bruce, Superintendent to the British Indian Government of the tea plantations in Assam (quoted in Fry, 'Facts and Evidences,' p. 33), is equally emphatic. He says:—'I might here observe that the British

'Government would confer a lasting blessing on the Assamese
'and the new settlers, if immediate and active measures were
'taken to put down the cultivation of opium in Assam, and
'afterwards to stop its importation by levying high duties on
'opium. If something of this kind is not done, and done
'quickly too, the thousands that are about to emigrate from
'the plains into Assam will soon be infected with the opium
'mania: that dreadful plague which has depopulated this
'beautiful country, turned it into a land of wild beasts, and
'has degenerated the Assamese from a fine race of people to
'the most abject, servile, crafty, and demoralised race in
'India. ... Few but those who have resided long in this
'unhappy country know the dreadful and immoral effects
'which the use of opium produces on the natives ... Would
'it not be the highest of blessings if our humane and en-
'lightened government would stop these evils with a single
'dash of the pen, and save Assam from the dreadful results
'attendant on the habitual use of opium?'

The despatches of Captain Elliott to Lord Palmerston, though full of passages condemning the trade, may perhaps be objected to as referring rather to the manner in which the traffic was then conducted, and not so much to the inherent evil effects of the drug itself. But no such objection can be urged against the testimony of Sir Thomas Wade or Sir Rutherford Alcock, and we find the former thus replying to the contention of Messrs. Jardine & Co. in his important memorandum relative to the revision of the Treaty of Tientsin:—'I cannot endorse the opinion of Messrs. Jardine, 'Matheson and Co., "that the use of opium is not a curse, 'but a comfort and a benefit to the hard-working Chinese." 'As in all cases of sweeping criticism, those who condemn 'the opium trade may have been guilty of exaggeration. ...
'It is impossible to deny that we bring them [the Chinese] 'that quality [of the drug] which, in the south at all events,

'tempts them the most and for which they pay dearest. It
'is to me vain to think otherwise of the use of the drug in
'China than as of a habit many times more pernicious,
'nationally speaking, than the gin and whisky drinking which
'we deplore at home. It takes possession more insidiously
'and keeps its hold to the full as tenaciously. I know no
'case of radical cure. It has ensured in every case within
'my knowledge the steady descent, moral and physical, of the
'smoker, and it is so far a greater mischief than drink, that it
'does not by external evidence of its effect expose its victim
'to the loss of repute which is the penalty of habitual
'drunkenness.'

Sir Rutherford before the East India Finance Committee in 1871 stated:—'I have no doubt that where there is a 'great amount of evil there is always a certain danger of 'exaggeration, but looking to the universality of the belief 'among the Chinese that whenever a man takes to smoking 'opium it will probably be the impoverishment and ruin of 'his family, a popular feeling which is universal both among 'those who are addicted to it, and who always consider 'themselves moral criminals, and amongst those who abstain 'from it and are merely endeavouring to prevent its con-'sumption, it is difficult not to conclude that what we hear of 'it is essentially true, and that it is a source of impoverish-'ment and ruin to families.' It may perhaps be objected that Sir Rutherford has lately changed his opinion on this matter, and that therefore he is not here an authoritative witness. It certainly is true that ten years' residence not in China but in England has led him to adopt another view, but as he is here mainly bearing witness to acknowledged facts, his authority is not greatly lessened.

Two more opinions of recent date may be added as bringing the matter up to the present time. Of these perhaps the incidental testimony of a distinguished opponent claims

the first place. It is that of the Marquis of Hartington, who in the last Opium Debate on June 4, 1881, argued against the abolition of the Bengal monopoly on the ground that our dominions in India would be flooded with cheap opium 'to the demoralisation of our own subjects,' apparently quite oblivious of the fact that the same objection might be urged against the existing system on behalf of the Chinese government. The second witness is Sir John Pope Hennessy, Governor of Hong Kong, who at the late Social Science Congress [in 1882] recognised in the opium trade a case of state-created crime, and, after denouncing in strong terms the crime arising from the opium smuggling which has its great focus in Hong Kong, went on to say :—' The British
' officials in China and India, and the opium merchants, are
' constantly asserting that the smoking of opium does not
' injure the health of the Chinese, . . . but the real objection
' of the governing classes and of the people of China to
' opium has been hardly noticed—namely, that it injures the
' intellect and impairs the moral character. Such is the
' objection that the Grand Secretary, Li Hung Chang, the
' virtual Prime Minister of China, over and over again re-
' peated to me. . . . I have constantly observed that whilst
' opium smoking may not injure the physique of some indi-
' viduals, it invariably deteriorates the moral character and
' increases crime. The crime arising from opium smoking
' it is not easy to repress. . . . The responsibility of creating
' and spreading such crime in a nation of 300,000,000,
' against the earnestly expressed wishes of the Empress
' Regent and her ministry, and indeed the wishes of the whole
' *literati* of China, is a responsibility that I trust England
' may soon be able to shake off.'

Next to these official testimonies may now be considered the evidence of medical men who have not or have resided in China. Among the first division prominence must be given to the opinion of Sir Benjamin Brodie, which was also endorsed by twenty-four of our leading medical men. It runs as follows:—' However valuable opium may be when 'taken as an article of medicine, it is impossible for any one 'who is acquainted with the subject to doubt that its habitual 'use is productive of the most pernicious consequences, 'destroying the healthy action of the digestive organs, weak-'ening the powers of the mind as well as those of the body, 'and rendering the individual who indulges in it a worse than 'useless member of society. I cannot but regard those who 'promote the use of opium, as an article of luxury, as inflicting 'a most serious injury on the human race.'—B. C. Brodie.

Sir James Risdon Bennett declares that 'it is not the 'less true that opium is a dangerous poison, and not the 'less pernicious because when taken habitually its action is 'very insidious.' The testimony of those medical men who have actually practised in China is, with the exceptions previously quoted on the other side, so almost unanimously against the view of the opium merchants, that one or two only need be placed in the witness-box.

Dr. Hobson, medical missionary at Canton, in a letter to Sir John Bowring (Parl. Pap. on Opium, 1842–1856, p. 42), says:—' I do not and cannot regard the use of opium by the ' Chinese as a matter of little importance. I must pronounce ' it a great and growing evil, the alleviation of which every ' true philanthropist must desire and rejoice to see.'

Dr. D. W. Osgood, an American medical missionary, says: —' After a residence of more than ten years in China, and ' after treating about 50,000 Chinese patients, of whom 1758 ' were treated for opium smoking, I wish to record my ' conviction that the use of opium is an unparalleled curse ; ' that its effect in every instance is to diminish vitality and ' to shorten life. . . In time the smoker becomes emaciated, ' and incapable of performing either continued mental or

'physical exertion. The Chinese themselves, after more
' than a century's experience and observation, universally
' condemn its use. Every rule has its exceptions, and
' occasionally we meet with those who have used opium for
' twenty or thirty years with but little apparent injury, but
' they are the exceptions and not the rule.'

Dr. Dudgeon, of Pekin, says (Ch. Recorder, Jan. 1869, p. 181, Feb. 1867, p. 204, quoted in Moule, 'Opium Question,' p. 56):—'Opium is the most mischievous of all sub-
' stances ever resorted to as a stimulant. It is externally
' more decent than ardent spirits in its results. A casual
' observer might walk through China, like Sir H. Pottinger,
' and see little or nothing of opium smoking. One requires
' to come into contact with the people, either officially,
' medically, or otherwise, to know the extent, strength, and
' evil of the system.'

Dr. L. Porter Smith, late of Hankow, author of the Chinese
' Materia Medica,' to conclude with his testimony, says:—
' I wish to place on record that after an intimate acquaint-
' ance with the people, the literature, the language, and the
' commerce of the large provinces of Central China, I am
' compelled to describe the infatuation, the miserable satu-
' ration of the country, the " change of type " of the character
' of the nation, and the miseries wrought upon individual
' habit, constitution, temper, and future, all exhibited in the
' course and consequences of the vice of opium smoking in
' China, as forming a unique instance of national lunacy and
' suicide. No epidemic possession of any people or sects
' reads in such terrible details as are afforded by the simple
' story of this horror. At the same time I protest against
' gratuitous exaggeration being imported into the question,
' now able to take care of itself.'

Between these medical testimonies and the few which have been quoted in favour of the opium trade, there certainly is some conflict. But if weight of authority and a numerical majority be allowed in such a case to turn the scale, there can be no doubt as to which side it will incline. Those who refuse to admit this course can only explain the inconsistency by admitting that the evil effects of opium, as of most other things, appear in different lights to different observers, and they must at least admit that the opinions of those who would minimise the evils are not expressed with the same confidence, and do not wear the same air of candour and truth, as the forcible statements of their opponents.

But if the position of Messrs. Jardine and Co. is almost wanting in Chinese and weak in medical support, is it not a suggestive fact that they have not strengthened it by the testimony of the many missionaries now working in China, whose evidence should, *prima facie*, carry much more than ordinary weight? And this for several reasons. The pursuit of their sacred calling necessarily gives them an intimate knowledge of, and brings them into unusually close connection with, the people among whom they sojourn. It cannot but afford them special opportunities of observing the daily life of the Chinese in their homes and families, and in many ways enable them to form a more accurate judgment, as to the inner life of the nation and the habits of the people, than persons in a more official position. Their profession, moreover, vouches for the truth of their statements, and while it enjoins them to promote everything that may tend to increase the morality, welfare, and godliness of the people, it equally orders them to denounce without fear or favour any proceedings likely to have the contrary effect. And further, as they are of the same nationality as the opium merchants, they cannot help wishing to place the conduct of their fellow-countrymen in the most favourable light possible. Consequently when we find the evidence of this important body of witnesses absolutely unanimous in condemning the practice of opium smoking as an unmitigated evil, positively and very extensively injurious to the Chinese, we are bound, even if we had hitherto been convinced of its truth, to pause before we assert, with Messrs. Jardine and Co., the benefits of the drug. Where testimony is so unanimous, to quote from one is to quote the opinions of all. Dr. Williamson, a well-known missionary and traveller in China for the past ten years, states (North China Daily News, Nov. 28, 1873, quoted by Moule, p. 59), that in his opinion 'opium without controversy does undermine the health, sap- 'ping the physical strength and blighting the moral sense of 'several tens of millions, to speak within the mark, in this 'country.'

With this we bring the case to an end, and await the verdict of our readers on the question at issue. Those, it is believed, who have carefully followed the testimonies on both sides will have little hesitation in concluding that, while there are undoubtedly instances in which the effects are not immediately or perceptibly injurious, still in the majority of cases the evil results cannot be gainsaid. Nor can they contend that, when the acknowledged evils of the drug are great and widespread, the few instances in which it is comparatively innocuous are sufficient to excuse the English government in its continued protection of the trade, or that the hostile attitude of the Chinese government is not amply justified.

This may introduce the second plea, which some would urge in extenuation, namely, that the Chinese have not been sincere in their prohibitory policy, and that in 1839 they wished to stay the 'oozing out of sycee silver' rather than to preserve the morality of their people.

And here it must be conceded at the outset that the *prima facie* evidence for this contention is strong, nor can it be maintained that the Chinese government are free from blame in this matter. At the same time careful examination will perhaps show that their shortcomings have been much more their misfortune than their fault, and calm consideration will make it pretty clear that so far from being a palliation it is rather an aggravation of our misdoings in the matter. The contention of Chinese insincerity is chiefly founded on two distinct features in their action towards the opium trade. First, the lax and utterly futile manner in which the stringent edicts of the Chinese government were not enforced previously to the Treaty of Tientsin; second, the extent to which of late years the growth and cultivation of opium in China has been connived at, if not actually encouraged. It certainly was an open and notorious fact that, previously to the years 1836 and 1837, while Imperial edicts were continually issued prohibiting the trade, the Chinese 'extortionate underlings' undisguisedly and shamelessly connived at their infraction, and readily accepted the bribes which were offered to them by the opium smugglers. To some extent indeed they quite justified the statements openly made, ' that opium, though 'contraband, paid its fixed fees with the same regularity 'as other articles paid their duties' (Lindsay, 'Is the War with China Just?'); that all, even the highest functionaries, not only connived at, but participated in the profits of, the trade; that 'it was a notorious fact that the 'appointments at Canton were considered to be the most 'lucrative in the whole empire, mainly on account of the 'opium trade, and that the Hoppo at Canton was usually a 'member of the Imperial house sent to Canton to reap his 'share of the golden harvest.' In addition to these disgraceful proceedings of the Chinese officials, it was also remarked as a curious coincidence that the commencement of vigorous proceedings against the importation and sale of the drug, coincided with the time when the balance of trade went against the Chinese, and thus necessitated a continued drain of sycee silver. *Prima facie* the Chinese authorities here appear to be on the horns of a dilemma. If the trade was as they maintained harmful and injurious, they must be convicted of encouraging it for the sake of the dishonest gains to be made from it; if the trade was innocuous in its effects, they must be equally found guilty of using morality as a mere pretext to call off attention from their other evil practices. In either case they must forfeit all claim on our sympathy.

When however the matter is scrutinised it appears in rather a different light. We then find that a strong line of distinction must be drawn between the action of the Imperial government and that of the provincial authorities and the minor officials who in China habitually ignore the orders of the supreme government as far as possible. But the extreme venality and readiness for corruption was no doubt largely due to that inherent defect of Chinese administration—the practice which universally prevails of paying officials insufficient salary. Such a system of executive arrangement would seriously hamper the efforts of any government. But in China, where the bonds of morality are often relaxed, and the decentralisation of the administrative system extreme, such a state of things was fraught with the most dangerous and fatal consequences. And to make matters worse, the years which witnessed this development of the opium trade were unfortunately years in which the Imperial authority was much weakened by other causes. For the successors of the able Emperor Kien-Lung were weak and feeble, and allowed the glory of the house to pass away and grow dim. Kea-King, his son and successor, was a worthless prince, wholly incapable of grappling with the evils of the situation. Tau Kwang, who succeeded Kea-King, though better than his father, was a man of but moderate ability, lacking that force of character and energy which alone could carry out the reform of the administration, and the other vital changes necessary for the extinction of the traffic. Still his earnest attempt to extinguish it in 1839 must at least be set down to his credit, while his continued refusal to legalise the trade in spite of the pressure of England, together with the destruction of the £3,000,000 sterling by Commissioner Lin, at least make doubtful his alleged insincerity. These considerations will probably supply many minds with some reasons for a less harsh verdict on the Chinese inaction before the opium war of 1839. Nor can the fact that we incited the Chinese officials to a dishonest neglect of their own laws, and corrupted them by the lavish bribes that we found it profitable to give, any more palliate our moral guilt than, to use Sir Wilfrid Lawson's simile, the co-operation of a dishonest footman can exonerate a housebreaker from the crime of burglary. For the impotence and inactivity of the Chinese after the war we are surely chiefly responsible. When we saw the Chinese had at length determined to crush the baneful traffic, our ignoble and unmanly protection of the trade, and the violence with which we chastised the honest action of the Chinese, evidently cowed them. Our shot and shell made it pretty clear that England was determined to take the traffic under the ægis of her protection, and the Chinese drew the natural inference that any new attempt to put it down would only result in new complications and a renewed collision with the foreigners—a contingency which, like the burnt child, they feared to experience a second time. But that the ruling spirits of the Empire had not faltered in their opinion with regard to the evils of the trade is apparent from their obstinate refusal to legalise it, 'to place a value on riches, and to slight men's lives,' in spite of the repeated and pressing 'representations' of the British residents.

Into the exact attitude of the Chinese towards the trade at the negotiations which resulted in its legalistion at Shanghai in November, 1858, or into the precise degree of direct or indirect compulsion exerted by the British guns or the British negotiators, it is unnecessary to enter. For, in spite of the strange contention emphasised by the Indian Government in their latest despatch, ' that Indian opium was neither forced ' upon the Chinese at the time the Treaty of Tientsin was ' concluded, nor was it forced upon them now,' it is impossible to ignore the testimony to the contrary of Sir Thomas Wade, whose knowledge of the matter must necessarily be more accurate than that at the disposal of the Indian Council. Sir Thomas Wade asserts (in his Memorandum on the revision of the Treaty of Tientsin) that ' the concessions made to us ' have from first to last been extorted against the conscience of ' the nation; in defiance, that is to say, of the moral convictions ' of its educated men ... of the millions who are saturated ' with a knowledge of the history and philosophy of their ' country;' a testimony which is most amply confirmed by Sir Rutherford Alcock in his evidence before the East India Finance Committee of 1871. The fact that the Chinese Commissioners, almost in the presence of our guns, at any rate with the echoes still ringing in their ears, made no objection to the admission of the drug into the legal tariff, if indeed they did not actually propose its insertion, can carry but little weight against such evidence. As however it is the only argument that can be produced in support of their contention, it is perhaps hardly surprising that the Government of India consider it ' a conclusive answer to the charge that the clause ' of the Tientsin Treaty under which opium was admitted into ' China was extorted from the Chinese.' Since that time, though the trade has been on a legal footing, we do not find that its new status commends it much more to the favourable notice of Chinese statesmen. The national conscience of England, if indeed in this matter she can be said to have any conscience at all, may perhaps have been quieted by the cloak of law and order that has been thrown over the conspicuous mischiefs of the trade, but the Chinese rulers are as anxious as ever to check its importation. At the revision of the Treaty of Tientsin in 1869 they so earnestly requested an increase in the prescribed duty that Sir Rutherford Alcock adopted their view and arranged for a higher duty. The English Government, however, 'though not free from doubt,' declined to ratify the proposal, and it consequently fell through. Again, in the Convention of Chefoo, which, though concluded six years ago, is still (October, 1882) unratified, arrangements calculated to hinder the importation and to check the smuggling of the drug were the main compensation they required for increased commercial privileges and other concessions yielded in that agreement. Nor is the clause in the treaty between America and China, which prohibits the import of opium under the American flag, a 'mere piece of hypocrisy,' but it plainly shows the direction in which Chinese official opinion concerning the trade is still tending. Finally, attention may be directed to a letter from Li Hung Chang, the Grand Secretary and Viceroy of China, which appeared in the *Times* of July 29th, 1881, and is quoted on p. 11 (note) of the recent Indian despatch. He there states:—' I ' may assert here, once for all, that the single aim of my ' government in taxing opium will be in the future, as in the ' past, to repress the traffic . . . never the desire to gain ' revenue from such a source. If it be thought that China ' countenances the import from the revenue it brings, it should ' be known that my government will gladly cut off all such ' revenue in order to stop the import of opium.' To some people, however, this avowed hostility to the opium traffic is hardly consistent with the extended growth and cultivation of opium in China, a practice which, if not encouraged, at least is not hindered by the authorities. The extent of the inconsistency, however, is more apparent than real. In the first place, by far the largest cultivation is carried on in the three provinces, Yunnan, Szechuen, and Manchuria, which are most distant from the centre of government, and where the executive has the least authority and influence. In the same direction the observations of the Indian Government in the recent despatch (p. 11), stating that there is a constant struggle going on between the imperial and provincial governments, would seem to point and to strengthen the inference that the admitted extension of the opium cultivation is due less to the imperial than to the subordinate authorities. Nor is it wholly improbable that the action complained of is to some extent due to a desire to benefit the people of China. For there is no small testimony that the native article is less mischievous in its effects than the Indian drug, and therefore if the Chinese, as is so persistently asserted, 'must have opium,' it is at least probable that the authorities prefer the consumption of the native drug instead of the Indian varieties. It is also quite open to Chinese statesmen to devise, if possible, a control over the trade; an object which can only be obtained by driving the Indian drug out of the market by an increased supply of the home production; while the most obvious worldly wisdom may perhaps by this time have taught the Chinese to prefer being poisoned for their own benefit to being poisoned for the benefit of any one else. If then either of these considerations are at all operative on the Chinese, we can only admit to our sorrow that in the same degree we are responsible for the impetus which has lately been given to the cultivation of the poppy in China.

On these two points then, by far the most important of those which may be urged as some excuse for our own conduct, the defence attempted would seem not only to have wholly failed, but to have proved actually an aggravation of our injustice and wrongdoing.

The two other points raised hardly require so complete or so lengthy a discussion, for their inherent insufficiency is apparent upon the least examination. The argument that we have made a good use of the revenues thus unjustly obtained, or the contention that the millions we have raised by pandering to the 'vicious luxury' of a distant people have been nobly dispensed in keeping the peace of India, in developing its resources, in introducing reforms, and educating the youthful population, is wholly beside the question at issue. In ordinary life it is no valid answer to a charge of forgery or embezzlement to plead that the funds so obtained have been applied to useful or benevolent purposes. Nor can we admit that the transactions of nations, and their dealings one towards another, may be judged by a lower standard than we recognise in our every-day life among each other, nor can the improvement of India at the expense of the moral and material welfare of China in any degree deserve our approbation, or reflect any credit on those who are responsible for such a policy.

The remaining plea of those who would place the most favourable construction on our conduct may be dismissed with equally scant consideration; for it is the old argument of all who have traded on the vices and weaknesses of their fellow-men. There is no use, they say, in India giving up the traffic: the appetite exists, and if India did not supply its gratification, either other nations, Persia or the Portuguese, or the Chinese empire itself, would continue the supply, and China thus would not be benefitted, whilst we should lose our millions of the opium revenue. But, in the first place, the allegation may be disputed, at least if England retired from the evil business as she ought, and not only ceased herself, but helped China in her attempts to prevent other nations occupying the vacant place. At any rate the experiment might at least be tried, and under proper conditions, the chances of a successful issue are at least equal to the probabilities of the contrary result. But however this may be, such a defence in all questions of morality can carry no weight; and whatever its value from a mere financial point of view, when urged from a moral standpoint, its validity cannot for an instant be admitted, 'in any forum whatsoever of law or of conscience.'

But if the case for the defence has thus broken down on all points, and no sufficient cause has been shown why the condemnation incurred by a violation of the abstract principles of morality should not be fully pronounced against us, what shall we have to say in answer to those who, after examining the moral characteristics of the Chinese people, find in them an additional and special reason for arraigning our conduct in this matter? The Chinese people are, it is alleged, 'the very people to coerce, or to seduce whom should 'seem a wrong of the deepest dye.' And for this reason. They are, it is said, among all the nations of the earth a people in whom, speaking generally, the sentiments of morality and the powers of self-control are the weakest and most uncertain. In them the animal and sensuous elements of their nature are most fully developed, while their relish of momentary and immediate pleasures is particularly keen and regardless of after consequences, a combination of characteristics which renders them specially liable to, and unable to resist, any temptation that may be presented to them. Moreover, it is urged, they lack in a marked degree strength of character and vigour of purpose, while at the same time the dictates and obligations of religion exert but a loose and inadequate control over their thoughts and actions. If this is true of their national characteristics, and at least the history of the trade and the testimonies of those acquainted with China and her people present, nothing to the contrary, surely our wrong-doing must appear, if possible, still less defensible. For if it be admittedly a crime more heinous in degree to impose upon the weakness of a child and to entice him astray into the paths of wickedness, than it is to persuade a full-grown man possessing all his faculties to join in some wrongful act—surely it must on the same reasoning be wicked in an increased degree for a nation great and powerful as our own thus to take advantage of the weakness or the vice of a people whose feebleness and ignorance ought rather to have received our care and protection, than to have furnished us with an occasion for oppression and wrong. And if this contention is valid as regards the Chinese people, it possesses an added force when used in reference to our conduct towards the Chinese government. The special weaknesses of the Chinese character might have escaped our knowledge; the peculiar impotence of the Chinese executive, owing to the extreme venality of its subordinates, could not possibly have been unnoticed. On the contrary, the ready corruptibility of the minor Chinese officials was from the first a patent and undisputed fact, and it is equally indisputable that from the first we encouraged it, and determined to make use of it to the utmost for the express purpose of pushing the sale of our wares. Instead of co-operating with the Chinese authorities in their attempts to cope with the evil, as the dictates of a generous policy, to say nothing of morality, would have enjoined, we ostentatiously ranged ourselves on the side of the evil-doers, supported them with our ships, and threw over them the ægis of the British flag. Nay more, after thus making the suppression of smuggling, which at first was only difficult, practically impossible, we have had the assurance to reproach the government with the failure of their preventive service. Even to-day the Indian Government requires from the Chinese authorities 'satisfactory evidence of their ability to 'execute any fiscal laws they may promulgate'—i. e. to put down smuggling—before it is even prepared to consider any proposal that the Chinese may make for the increase of their import duties. When such has been, and practically still is, our conduct to China in this important part of our dealings with her; when we cannot disclaim complicity with desperadoes engaged in violating the decrees of their own government, or deny a forcible interference to protect them from the consequences of their illegal actions, it must be completely futile to argue in defence of our conduct from any moral considerations. For to sum up, the case against us stands as follows:—We have admittedly transgressed the cardinal principles of morality as they are commonly understood between man and man, between nation and nation. The several pleas we have urged as affording if not some justification at least some excuse and palliation of our conduct, though possessing a *prima facie* plausibility and some apparent force, have yet proved on further examination to be unsupported by facts and deficient in cogency. Finally, in one important particular, aggravating circumstances have been brought forward against us, the relevance of which we are unable to dispute, and the truth of which we are, unfortunately for our fair fame and national reputation, unable to disprove or to rebut.

Such in brief is the conclusion which an examination of the question in its moral bearings compels us to accept. For the honour of England, for the good name of our countrymen, it were greatly to be wished that a different decision were possible. But the facts are too clear and the deductions from them too unassailable—indeed they have virtually proved too strong for the able apologist of our policy who has recently stated the case on behalf of the government of India in the important despatch which has already been referred to. Even he is compelled to admit that nothing can be urged against the abstract principles laid down by Mr. Pease in his speech in Parliament on June 4th, 1880, when 'he declined to judge our transactions with the 'Chinese in reference to this matter by the low standard 'of the financial wants of the East Indian Government,' and asserted that 'as a Christian nation we must deal with this 'question on certain laws laid down by that Gospel in which 'almost every one in the country believed, by the high moral 'law, and by the international law which was observed among 'civilised nations.' But, while admitting the unassailable strength of this position, the despatch goes on to say:—'The 'difficulties of the problem have to be fairly faced. The 'hard facts of the case, whether from the Chinese or the 'Indian point of view, have to be borne in mind. These 'facts can neither be altered, nor can their significance be 'attenuated by any enunciation of abstract principles.' Is not this a convenient periphrasis for asserting that in the present case the defence on moral grounds cannot be maintained, that the great principles of right and wrong must yield to the considerations of practical expediency? In 'other 'words, that in this matter the claims of Christian morality 'and international equity must be set aside in the interests of 'the Indian revenue.'

Merely to protest against such a contention would in this age be a hardly sufficient answer. For though public opinion has of late years made considerable advance in its conceptions of moral questions, still it has not yet been educated sufficiently to act on the abstract belief that

'To do the right because it is the right
'Is noble in the scorn of consequence,'

or to refuse an immoral advantage simply and solely on account of its immorality. It is therefore necessary to show, if possible, that a course of policy which is admittedly inconsistent with the principles of morality and the rules of right conduct has been and still is contrary to practical expediency; that it is unjustifiable on the very grounds on which alone its defence can be attempted. The difficulties in the way of entering on a new course of policy are naturally considerable and complicated—the more so by reason of our long persistence in wrong-doing. Still it is hoped that they can be shown to be not insurmountable, and that the satisfactory settlement of this vexed question is not so far out of the region of practical politics as the Government of India apparently would have us believe.

CHAPTER III.

THE EXPEDIENCY OF THE TRAFFIC.

ANY discussion of the comparative expediency or inexpediency of our connection with the Opium Traffic obviously divides itself into two distinct parts—(1) as regards our Indian Empire, (2) as it affects or has affected our commercial intercourse and our political relations with China and the Chinese. Further, each of these divisions will naturally include an enquiry into its results in the past, and, perhaps more particularly for our purpose, an estimate of the effects which may be expected to result from its working in the future.

First, then, with regard to its past influence on our Indian empire. Viewing it retrospectively, it must be confessed that hitherto our connection with this traffic, a traffic apparently so unholy and immoral, so far from bringing down curses on our Indian empire, would rather appear to have altogether blessed it. Its results have been financially magnificent. The revenue it provides for India has grown from one and a half millions in 1840 to an average of seven millions at the present time, a sum which has been drawn from the pockets of a far-off people, and has been one principal element in that policy of developing the resources of India which has been so largely and so successfully carried out. Indeed it may almost be said that from the standpoint of mere expediency there are but two arguments which can be urged in qualification of its wholly beneficial influence on our Indian possessions. These are (1) the extent to which the cultivation of the drug may have been one of the causes of the recent famines, by occupying with the poppy some of the rich territories that would otherwise have been free for the cultivation of breadstuffs, and (2) the degree in which the substantial assistance of the opium revenue may have encouraged among Indian statesmen an unsafe system of financial management, by inducing too much reliance on its aid in making good any deficiencies in the budget estimate, and thus discouraging the practice of that rigid economy, which the poor and undeveloped condition of the country must for many years to come imperatively demand. The force however of the first of these two arguments is not great. 'Forty-nine years out of fifty Bengal grows rice and 'food enough to feed herself and to export an enormous 'balance; while the profits from the opium trade can pur-'chase from Burmah three times the amount of corn that 'can be grown on the space now occupied in opium cultiva-'tion.' The cogency of the other consideration is too speculative and uncertain to carry much weight in a practical discussion of the question. At the same time it may be said that the hint it contains should not be wholly disregarded by the rulers of India: more especially as there is an impression (vide *Times*, Feb. 15, 1879) that the improvement of public works, i. e. the development of the country, would have been more earnestly attended to but for the easy way of getting revenue which the opium monopoly has provided.

But however this may be, the advantages of the opium trade to India, from a mere expediency standpoint, cannot be denied. Nor can it be maintained that its beneficial results as regards India have been illusory. But for the future the prospect is not so reassuring. Already some think they can discern upon the horizon of our opium gains the little cloud like unto a man's hand, which may in the perhaps not far distant future involve the prosperity of the country in storms and thick darkness. For, to abandon metaphor, there can hardly be a doubt that China, as already noticed, has herself taken up the cultivation of the poppy, and that consequently the exclusion of the Indian drug from the Chinese market may only be a question of time. It is no doubt true that the action of the Chinese is not everywhere uniform, but the broad fact that the native cultivation is widely extending can hardly be disputed. Indeed, the Indian Government in the despatch already referred to (p. 23), clearly states that the consumption of opium and the area of cultivation of the poppy in China are rapidly increasing. This contingency has indeed been more and more prominent in the trade reports annually issued by our consuls at the treaty ports, while the evidence in its support on p. 29 of the despatch is so valuable that some quotations may here be offered to the reader. The consul at Canton, writing on June 22, 1881, says:—' The consumption ' of native opium is undoubtedly extending, especially among ' the lower classes ... Nothing is more likely to affect the ' price of Indian opium than the improvement and increase ' in the quality and quantity of the native article.' The report of the consul at New Chang, dated February 17, 1881, is still more serious. After stating that the quantity of Indian opium imported, all but a very small portion being Malwa, fell from 2302 chests in 1879 to 1156 chests in 1880, it goes on to say:—' This great decrease is chiefly due to the increased ' cultivation of the poppy in these provinces. The harvest ' last year was unusually good, and native opium was conse- ' quently so cheap that a further diminution of the Indian ' drug may confidently be expected in 1881. In fact it is ' expected that New Chang may ere long form a port of ex- ' port for opium to other parts of China.' To the same effect the consul at Tientsin, writing on November 10, 1880,

reports that 'there is a decrease of 1000 chests in Malwa, or
' about 30 per cent. There is also a marked decrease in
' Bengal, but Persian shows an increase of 150 chests. The
' sudden cessation of the demand for Malwa is partly due to
' the enhanced cost of the drug, but mainly to the native drug
' being so abundant this season in all opium-growing districts.
' Shansi is usually a great consumer of Bengal opium, but
' this year hardly any was sent there. The drug grown in
' Shansi is, as stated in my report on Persian opium, of ex-
' cellent quality, and the out-turn of the crop this year is
' expected to be large.' To these official reports the despatch
adds the important testimony of the *Hong Kong Daily News*
(as quoted in the *Times of India* of April 9, 1881):—'It
' is quite impossible to shut our eyes to the fact that the
' foreign drug is losing ground in the north of China. The
' area under poppy cultivation has extended immensely. The
' consumption of Indian opium has in consequence been
' almost reduced to nil in Chinkiang, and the New Chang
' correspondent of a contemporary says that that market is so
' glutted with native opium that the stock of Malwa has be-
' come a drug in more senses than one, and the day is
' approaching when native opium will become an article of
' export from the port.'

Ten years ago the same fact was beginning to make itself
apparent, and in 1872-73, Mr. Medhurst, our consul at
Shanghai, expressed his ' opinion '—an opinion borne out by
the principal opium merchants in Shanghai—'that we may
' look forward to a gradual falling off in the demand for the
' foreign drug, and if the cultivation of the poppy continues
' to spread as it is now doing, to the virtual extinction of
' the trade in Indian opium.'

According to Mr. Hughes, consul at Hankow, the mildness
of the native article is the principal cause of the growing pre-
ference for its use. ' The Chinese say that it is much easier

'to give up temporarily or abandon altogether the habit of
'smoking native, than that of smoking foreign, opium ...
'Foreign opium affects the system to such a degree that the
'sudden abandonment of the use of so powerful a drug would
'to a certainty impair the health; whereas the smoker of
'native opium is by no means so seriously affected by the
'want of his favourite narcotic.'

To sum up the facts of the matter as regards China, it will be best to quote the conclusions arrived at by Mr. Arthur Nicholson, Secretary of Legation at Pekin, who in February, 1878, drew up a careful report on the whole question, and concluded by directing attention to the following '*facts*.'

'1. That within the last few years the production of native 'opium has increased and is increasing. 2. That the poppy 'is cultivated in spite of prohibitory governmental edicts, and 'in most cases with the connivance of the authorities. 3. 'That the cultivation is likely to be further extended owing 'to the large profits which can be made from it. 4. That 'the native can easily undersell the foreign drug in the 'market. 5. That the chief and apparently the sole ad-'vantage possessed by the Indian drug over the native article 'lies in its superior quality.' The possibility therefore, that China may some day no longer require the Indian opium is by no means to be disregarded, and the gravity of such a contingency on our Indian revenue cannot be mistaken. Indeed before the East India Finance Committee of 1871, high Indian authorities, Sir Frederick Halliday, Sir Cecil Beadon, and Mr. Maitland, a well-known Indian merchant, fully recognised the fact, and admitted its importance as affecting the Indian revenue. At the same time it must not be hidden that there are names of authority on the other side. Vice-Consul Baber, writing from Kew Kiang, after admitting the extended cultivation of the native drug, says, 'it is im-'probable that the native growth will ever seriously affect the

'consumption of the Indian import. Once accustomed to
'the superior flavour and potency of the latter, no opium
'smoker would dream of preferring the native variety, which
'in fact is employed almost exclusively for purposes of adul-
'teration, or consumed by the poorer classes, and relinquished
'even by them the moment they can afford the higher price
'of the Indian drug.' Again, in his report on opium in the
western provinces of China, written in 1880, and quoted in
the recent despatch of the Indian Government, he says:—
'Indian opium has probably more to hope than to fear from
'the contest of prices. Its position is moreover rendered
'almost unassailable by its hitherto unrivalled mellowness, a
'quality which the best Yunnan variety can only acquire by
'several years keeping .... Hitherto no kind of native opium
'combining strength with superior mellowness has appeared
'in the market. But'—and does not this admission greatly
weaken the foregoing argument—'within the last few years
'Kan-suh has produced a new competitor which is universally
'pronounced by competent smokers to be in both respects
'superior even to Malwa opium.' Before the East India
Finance Committee of 1871, Mr. Winchester, formerly Consul
at Shanghai, thought that the Indian drug would still maintain its position in the Chinese market, and that the demand
for it would increase as it always had done. Mr. Laing also,
who has been finance minister in India, held that the opium
revenue was perfectly safe, and that India had nothing to
fear from Chinese opium.

While therefore the evidence is too conflicting to allow an
absolutely definite answer, yet it would appear that there is
more ground for a desponding than for an optimistic view of
the position. At any rate, all must agree with Sir Richard
Temple, when, in his Budget Estimate for 1872-73, he told
us that 'year by year experience brings home to convic-
'tion that there are few points of greater consequence to

'the prosperity of Indian finance than a safe and moderate
'estimate of the opium revenue.' And yet the latest Indian
Budget can show a brilliant balance sheet, and make considerable remissions through a successful year of opium
profit. In the face of experience such as this it almost
seems like courting the fate of Cassandra to hint that this
good-fortune may not always continue, and to prophesy that
one day perhaps, not so far distant, the balance will be
placed by the opium revenue on the other side of the Indian
financial statement. In face of such surpluses it may seem
impertinent if not absurd to urge the inexpediency of such a
source of revenue: nevertheless we are constrained to insist
upon it. Whether our imperfect vision can see it or not, the
fact remains, that the fundamental laws of right or wrong
cannot for ever be violated with impunity; and though the
day of reckoning may be long postponed, yet it will assuredly not be postponed for ever. We have only to read
history aright to learn that this has always been true, and
'that each great catastrophe in the history of nations is in
'some way or other the consequence of injustice.' And
merely to urge that, because we cannot see the evil day approaching, it will never overtake us, is to assert an omniscience
and an infallibility for which we can have neither warrant nor
excuse. It is rather our duty to believe 'that this great God's
'world has verily, though deep beyond our soundings, a just
'law: that our part is to conform to that law, and in devout
'silence to follow it, not questioning, but obeying it as un-
'questionable;' and we may be well assured that if we thus
act we shall not be disappointed in the consequent result.

Still vague prognostications of distant disasters can hardly
be expected to weigh overmuch with statesmen who have
found the actual results so advantageous. Nor is it sufficient
to urge mere abstract considerations when 'the opinion of
'those who for the time being are responsible for the conduct

'of Indian finances,' is, to quote the words of their recent communication, 'that the Government of India is quite un-'able to devise any means by which the loss of the revenue, 'consequent on the suppression of the poppy cultivation in 'Bengal, could be recouped, and that until such means be 'devised, the loss of the Bengal opium revenue would result 'in the normal annual expenditure of the Government being 'greater than its receipts; that is to say, that India would be 'insolvent;' when, moreover, they solemnly warn us 'that any 'present attempt to abandon the opium revenue, whilst con-'ferring a very doubtful benefit on the population of China, 'would do incalculable harm to the 250 millions of people 'over whom we rule in India,' it certainly seems necessary to pause for a while and consider. If indeed this deliberate conclusion be well founded, if the opium revenue is financially necessary to secure the well-being of the peoples for whom we are now responsible in India, we are certainly in a serious dilemma. On the one side we are bound by every moral consideration not to sacrifice the natives of India by surrendering the yearly profit from the opium trade, and consequently to continue a manifest injustice on the Chinese peoples: on the other hand we are equally bound by moral considerations to abandon the revenue and thus to inflict serious injury on our Indian subjects. Or to put the matter in other words, we are forced to conclude, 'that the Indian Government is 'bound by considerations of justice, morality, and humanity, 'as far as India is concerned, but is not bound by them be-'yond the ocean, or on the other side of the Himalayas.' This, however, is a palpable *reductio ad absurdum*, forcibly suggesting that the fundamental premiss is erroneous, and that the financial position which the Indian Government have so carefully taken up is not wholly impregnable. Nor is such an inference improbable upon other grounds. The notorious conflict between the opposing schools of Indian financial economists, those who with the Stracheys believe liberally in the 'elasticity' of the Indian revenue, or those who agree with Mr. Fawcett and take a much gloomier view of the financial situation, shows that the conditions of Indian finance are not yet known with sufficient certainty. But apart from such general considerations, the budget of the present year affords at least some reason for doubting the alleged absolute necessity of the opium revenue. For when we find that it shows a surplus of nearly three millions sterling, it is an obvious inference that, for the present year at all events, a diminution of the opium revenue to that amount would not have imperilled the financial solvency of India. Nor does the disposition of the surplus at all weaken this conclusion. For it appears that the two items of revenue which are to receive the benefit are items in which the need of reduction was, to say the least, not absolutely imperative. Indeed, as the *Times* correspondent remarked, they were surprises, wholly unexpected in India. The salt duty no doubt is one distasteful to our English ideas, but the natives of India have not clamoured loudly for its reduction, while it can hardly be denied, that the remission of the import duties on cotton goods was made much more to retain the support of the Lancashire manufacturers, than in the interests of the Hindoos, if indeed the rights of the latter were not rather postponed to the interests of the former. But cogent as this reasoning may be as regards the present year, it may be urged that it affords no argument against the conclusions of the Government in years of less financial success. It is therefore necessary to examine into the matter more closely, and to discover, if possible, the exact relation in which the opium revenue stands to the financial stability of India. According to paragraph 55 of the Indian Government's Despatch:—'The average net revenue derived from the sale 'of Bengal opium during the last ten years is £4,357,000. 'During the last three years the average revenue has been

'£5,450,000.' In dealing with a fluctuating revenue of this sort it is difficult to speak with accuracy, but we shall perhaps be not very far from the mark if we assume that the abandonment of the revenue derived from opium in Bengal would cost about £5,000,000. Accepting then this estimate of the loss which would be incurred; in what way may we hope to make it good? In the conflict and uncertainty both of opinions and of knowledge on this matter, it is certainly not easy to give a definite answer. It has been urged by some authorities, that, excluding the opium revenue and the expenditure on public works, the Indian financial statement has always had a balance on the right side. Consequently, say these critics, the one thing needful to promote a financial equilibrium, is to check expenditure on public works. To those who object that this would be sacrificing the welfare of India to China, it may perhaps be pointed out that, as no person can claim a benefit at the expense of another, so the populations of India cannot demand that their advantage should be sought if it involves the injury of the Chinese people.

As to the possibility of imposing increased or new taxes, the present Finance Minister and his predecessor appear to have held diametrically opposite opinions to those stated in the recent despatch. Sir John Strachey and his brother, in their book on the 'Finances and Public Works of India,' assert that it would be quite feasible, and they say 'it could un-
' doubtedly be possible, to increase largely the income of the
' State without serious injury to the industry of the country,
' and without political danger, in the event of any great
' financial emergency, such for instance as might conceivably
' arise if we were suddenly to lose the greater part of our
' opium revenue, or if the difficulties caused by the fall in
' the value of silver in relation to gold should attain to any
' very alarming dimensions.' And again, 'There would be
' little difficulty in case of necessity, in almost immediately

'increasing the revenue by existing and other taxes of a
'little objectionable nature to the extent of at least £2,000,000
'per annum, and if a much larger sum than any which could
'be provided by such means, or by the growth of already
'existing revenues, should be required in consequence of some
'great financial catastrophe, the income of the State could
'certainly be increased by several millions a-year without
'injury to the country.' Such an opinion must be taken for
what it is worth, and of that a mere outsider can, of course,
form no valid estimate. It may however at least deserve
respectful consideration as the belief of administrators who
in their official capacities have had long and extensive knowledge of the subject, and no small share in shaping the
financial policy of India.

But, in addition to the possibilities of new taxation, they
have formed a high opinion of the elasticity and probable
expansion of all the great items of revenue. They state that
the net receipts from all sources have risen from £42,375,176
in 1869, to £49,431,000 in 1880-1, an increase of £7,055,824
during the eleven years, which shows the average increase is
more than £600,000 a-year. Sir Arthur Cotton, no mean
authority on Indian subjects, likewise insists most earnestly
on the favourable prospects of Indian finance, and he vehemently maintains 'that there is not a shadow of excuse for
'our continuing this trade of opium from its being necessary
'in point of finance.' He affirms 'the astonishing fact that
'we are perfectly independent of the opium revenue, having a
'clear surplus of three and a half millions without it, and that
'revenue increasing at the rate of half a million a-year.' He
therefore concludes that 'such is the state of the Indian
'finances that there is nothing whatever in the way of our at
'once prohibiting the cultivation of the plant. It is already
'forbidden in 95 per cent. of India, and it is only necessary
'to extend that prohibition to the remaining 5 per cent.'

On the other side must be placed the emphatic statement of the Indian Government as laid down in their recent despatch, thus:—'It cannot be too clearly understood, that, neither 'by any measure tending to develope the resources of the 'country, nor by an increase of taxation, which is practically 'within the range of possibility, nor by any reduction of 'expenditure, could the Government of India in any adequate 'way at present hope to recoup the loss which would accrue 'from the suppression of the poppy cultivation in Bengal.' Reviewing each branch of expenditure and source of revenue, they merely reiterate in changed phrases the *non possumus* they have formulated above. Coming from so high an authority such a conclusion must receive careful consideration. Moreover, on some points it is supported by the opinion of Mr. Fawcett; who at the same time differs as to the possibility of retrenchment and economy in expenditure and administration. In the disagreement of such high authorities an outsider must hold his peace; he would, however, just hint to the Indian Government that, even if it is impossible 'in any adequate degree to impose taxation or to 'retrench, it need not be impossible to make a commence-'ment in both directions.' And he would urge that even if the 'total suppression' of the opium manufacture would involve the insolvency of India, it does not necessarily follow that the partial suppression, or the trial of restriction, need have such disastrous effects. Indeed, it would seem that to argue with the Government of India that, because we cannot bring in the millennium to-day, we are to do nothing to hasten its coming, but merely to stand still and let matters go on as hitherto, is to adopt a contention unworthy of men placed in such a high and responsible position.

But after all, even granting to the full the *non possumus* of the Indian Council, and admitting without qualification their view of the position, the burden is merely shifted from India to Great Britain. And if this be necessary, it is at least not wholly unjustifiable. For the question is quite as much one of Imperial as of Indian policy. Not only did the British Government—or rather the British people through Parliament—become responsible for the trade by the resolution of 1832, 'that it does not deem it advisable to abandon so 'important a source of revenue;' but, to say nothing of the systematic protection of the trade, the instructions to its officials 'not to interfere with the undertakings of British ' subjects,' the fact that the British nation has twice sanctioned an appeal to arms, cannot but give increased force to the contention. And further, if we bear in mind the supreme authority which the English Parliament always assumes in the affairs of India, the argument that England should bear the loss arising from the suppression of the Bengal monopoly, if India cannot, becomes almost irresistible. Nor can the amount of compensation necessary in any degree weaken the obligation; for even if it did require much more than the £20,000,000 paid to the slave-owners of the West Indies, it may certainly be replied that the rapid expanse of our wealth makes the increased amount of but minor importance. And if England and India together can find the fifteen or sixteen millions required for the doubtful benefits of the Afghan war, without imperilling or seriously weakening the financial stability of India, it may well be contended that to find the money required to make good the loss of the opium revenue need not be more difficult or dangerous. Last of all, we would urge that the fair fame and reputation of any nation is not usually appraised in numerical figures, and is generally considered well worthy of considerable self-sacrifice. How much more then should this be the case with England—England, whose children claim to be the leaders of civilisation, nay, more—the very schoolmasters of the rest of the world in honour, integrity, and uprightness!

Should not such considerations as these in some way counterbalance the sordid and miserable pleas of financial expediency, and overcome the *non possumus* argument on which the Indian Government now takes its stand? Shall we as Englishmen be any longer willing to stand, as regards this matter, 'in a somewhat false and invidious position'? Shall we any longer connect ourselves with a traffic which brings upon us shame and reproach amongst the nations of the earth, and which cannot fail to provoke against us the righteous indignation of heaven? Shall we not rather 'shake 'off the responsibility of creating and spreading crime in a 'nation of three hundred millions, and by a speedy act of 'reparation, ere it is too late, atone for the past and determine 'to act more honourably in the future.' And though repentance may at first be difficult, yet we shall surely find that, even in political prosperity and in worldly welfare, 'the fear 'of the Lord, that is wisdom; and to depart from evil is under-'standing.'

But apart from the Indian side of the question, the material interests of England require some consideration at our hands. The predominance of our mercantile and manufacturing interests make the unhindered development of our commerce a matter of the first importance to our well-being as a nation; consequently, any influence which tends to narrow the limits or to increase the difficulties of our intercourse with foreign peoples in the same degree must incur our suspicion if not our condemnation. And that the opium trade comes under this category will hardly be questioned by any one who has attentively followed the history of the traffic as already set forth. But, even if the case were otherwise, it would not be a difficult task to show from general considerations that it is contrary to the true principles of a sound commercial economy. It is generally accepted as an economical maxim that every transaction is really advantageous only so far as it benefits equally both parties to the compact. Bargains such as those between Glaucus and Diomede,

χρύσεα χαλκείων ἑκατόμβοι' ἐννεαβοίων,

however much they may be sought after under the present low standard of commercial morality, can find no justification on the principles of a sound economy. And that such is the characteristic feature of our opium transactions with China is only too certain and undeniable. Few of its apologists seriously believe that opium confers any benefit upon its purchasers, the utmost they can maintain being that it does them no harm. Consequently, the inference is inevitable that the essential requisite of a beneficial commerce is absent in the case under discussion, and therefore an adverse verdict on mere economic principles cannot be resisted. But in addition to this fundamental unsoundness, in itself the opium trade must necessarily be adverse to all other commerce between foreign nations and China. It is obviously impossible for wealth to be expended on commodities which, even if not harmful, are at any rate unproductive, without curtailing the power of purchasing other and more beneficial wares. It is therefore absurd to suppose that the Chinese can spend annually, as estimated by Mr. Hart (of the Chinese Imperial Customs), £16,800,000 in opium, without very seriously limiting their power to purchase our cottons, woollens, and other manufactures. Therefore, if it be granted that the traffic is beneficial and profitable to India, it can only be so at the expense of our manufacturing and mercantile classes at home. In other words, the £8,000,000 of revenue which the opium trade pours into the coffers of our Indian Empire, is not drawn so much from the pockets of the Chinese as really deducted from the earnings of the British working man. But this is not the whole of the case against the trade: there is another consideration which must not be overlooked. The exclusive and suspicious character of the Chinese, and their extreme unwillingness to admit foreigners into the 'inner land' on anything like a footing of friendly reciprocity, are too well known to require either statement or proof in detail. At the same time it is at least a noteworthy fact that before the rise of the opium trade we possessed fuller facilities for commerce than at the time of Lord Napier's mission, when the trade had largely developed, and when, to use his own remarkable words, ' all the privileges formerly enjoyed by the British ' have been curtailed from time to time, till we are at this ' moment tied down under dreadful restrictions to the mere ' port of Canton.' That this policy of the Chinese was wholly justifiable need not be affirmed, but it may at least be asserted with confidence that our evil reputation as opium smugglers and open law-breakers has certainly furnished the Chinese with some reason for their restrictive and unfriendly policy. Its disadvantages to our commerce in any case would be manifest, but they are made still more obvious by a consideration of the general conditions of Chinese commerce. For there is a general consensus of opinion among those qualified to form a judgment on the matter, that freer intercourse and less restrained communication with the inhabitants of the country, together with additional facilities of access to new markets, are among the most indispensable requisites for a satisfactory increase of our trade with China. It has indeed been remarked of the Chinese by our Consul at Hankow (in his admirable Paper on the ' Conditions of Commercial Progress in China,' annexed to his trade report for the year 1870-71), that 'they will not advance towards ' foreigners to seek their trade till the foreigners have pressed ' it upon them. They will never themselves improve their ' means of transport, nor develope new wants like progressive ' nations. Foreigners must provide the means of bringing ' different parts of the Empire into close communication, and

'they must also to a certain extent create the wants which
'they wish to supply by "introducing" their goods to their
'customers. Commerce,' he adds, 'everywhere requires to
'be energetically pushed, and this is peculiarly true of the
'trade in foreign manufactures in China.' While all this is
noteworthy for its own sake, it seems to afford a strong
argument against the expediency of maintaining the close
connection now existing between the opium trade and
English commerce. For if foreigners desire to obtain from
the Chinese greater facilities of communication, they on their
side must be prepared to satisfy the advisers of the Emperor
that the wares in which they propose to deal will not prove
injurious to those of his subjects who may purchase them.
For it can hardly be expected that any government, and
least of all a government conducted as the Chinese on
paternal principles, should readily grant facilities to foreign
commerce which may result in the extension of a practice
which it has long regarded as injurious, and for the suppression of which it has not yet lost the desire.

If then the broad principles just discussed supply good
grounds for believing that the traffic is hurtful to our general
commerce, it may be worth while to enquire whether practical
experience and actual facts endorse or contradict the conclusions arrived at. On this point, it is believed, there will
be little disagreement. Sir John Bowring may indeed inform
Lord Clarendon, in reply to Lord Shaftesbury's memorial,
that 'no evidence exists to show that, but for the opium trade,
'British manufactures would have been more purchased;'
Messrs. Jardine, Matheson and Co. may at the same time
declare that 'the decline in cottons imported is due to other
'sources;' Messrs. Lindsay and Co. may profess their belief
that the lessened import is due to rebellion and anarchy;
nevertheless, the general consensus both of facts and opinions
is so greatly against them that such views must be disre-

garded, or at least only accepted with large qualifications. As Mr. Donald Matheson in his pamphlet says, the following figures plainly show that 'the effects of the opium trade on 'legal commerce have been most disastrous.' And this he proves by the following:—

'In the decade between 1845 and 1855, while our exports 'to all countries rose from £60,000,000 to £95,000,000, to 'India they rose from £6,700,000 to £10,900,000; to China 'they *fell* from £2,394,000 to £1,277,000, and our imports 'from that country rose from £5,500,000 to £8,500,000; 'and the opium import to China rose from £5,000,000 to '£8,000,000;' figures which, as Mr. Matheson contends, obviously point to only one conclusion, and clearly show that, 'in supplying the Chinese with an intoxicating drug, 'we are drying up their natural capacity to consume our 'manufactures.'

But the fact may be confirmed by other commercial statistics. We find that, according to Parliamentary Papers, during the years from 1803 to 1808 inclusive—years be it remembered which were virtually anterior to the rise of the opium trade—the average export of the East Indian Company to China in woollens alone amounted to £1,128,557 per annum. From 1811 to 1816 the total value of the exports of China averaged £895,954 per annum; from 1817 to 1822 £750,289; from 1823 to 1838 £709,759, thus showing for these years—years during which the opium trade was rapidly growing—a gradual diminution. Yet once more. The exports of British goods to China from 1834 to 1838 inclusive averaged rather more than £1,000,000 per annum, showing that during those years—years in which the China trade was open, and the illicit traffic in opium greatly developed—the whole annual shipments of British goods to China since the opening of the trade is not equal to the annual value of woollens alone sent to China during the first years of the century

(Fry, 'Facts and Evidences,' pp. 52 seqq.). As, moreover, the exports from China increased from £2,242,300 in 1827 to £5,102,347, it cannot be said that the unfavourable condition of English commerce is due to a diminution of trade in that direction. Consequently, the only inference left to us is that the undoubted development of the opium traffic during those years was mainly the cause of this reduced demand for British manufactures. And this was also the belief of persons at the time well qualified to form an opinion on the matter. The manufacturers of Leeds presented a petition on the subject, which states:—' That your
' petitioners have the strongest grounds for believing that
' the daring and systematic violation by the opium smugglers
' of the laws of China (laws enacted to preserve the health,
' happiness, and morals of the people) has exerted a most
' injurious influence on British interests; that it has been the
' occasion of frequent stoppages of trade, of restrictions and
' impediments to commerce, continually increasing in number
' and severity; and finally, that it has been the cause of the
' existing suspension of our friendly and commercial relations
' with that Empire, under circumstances which threaten to in-
' volve the nation in an unjust, dishonourable, and expensive
' war. That your petitioners believe that the dishonourable
' and immoral trade in opium is the means of preventing, to
' a great extent, an honourable and highly profitable trade
' in the woollens, cottons, and other manufactures of Great
' Britain, which would otherwise be introduced into that
' country in payment for the Chinese produce consumed here;
' and that the opium trade is thus injurious in a high degree
' to the manufacturing and mercantile classes, and to the
' general prosperity of the United Kingdom ' (Fry, 'Facts
' and Evidences,' p. 54).

Such testimony, however, though well-nigh conclusive on the matter, may perhaps be objected to as giving merely the home-view of the question, and consequently based on an inadequate knowledge of the facts. To obviate such an objection the following evidence from persons in China at the time, and peculiarly qualified to form a judgment, are added in its confirmation.

Captain Elliott, the British superintendent, writing in 1839 to Lord Palmerston, said,—'After the most deliberate re-'consideration of this course of traffic, I declare my own 'conviction that in its general effects it is intensely mis-'chievous to every branch of the trade.' And again, in February, 1837 (China Papers, 1840, p. 190), he says:—'It 'cannot be good that the conduct of a great trade should be 'so dependent upon the steady continuance of a vast pro-'hibited traffic, in an article of vicious luxury, high in price, 'and liable to frequent and prodigious fluctuation. In a 'mere commercial point of view, therefore, I believe it is 'susceptible of proof that the gradual diversion of British 'capital into other channels of employment than this would 'be attended with advantageous circumstances.' And if this was the opinions of the government officials, it was certainly that of those China merchants who were not themselves connected with the trade, as may be seen from the following letter (Fry, 'Facts and Evidences,' p. 44), written at Canton by a correspondent of an eminent Liverpool house, in which he says,—'The mischievous effects of this (opium) traffic in 'interfering with the importation of British manufactures, as 'well as of all descriptions of Indian produce other than the 'forbidden drug, in absorbing the capital and the attention 'of both native and foreign merchants, and in subjecting the 'whole foreign commerce to a system of jealous and vexa-'tious restrictions, can hardly be overestimated, and are most 'palpable to any one on the spot whose powers of observation 'are not impaired by prejudice or interest.'

Such testimonies as these, when joined to that afforded by

the cogent figures already given, may surely be accepted as an ample refutation of the vague inferences and negative assertions put forward by Sir John Bowring and the opium merchants already quoted. It may therefore be taken as an established fact, that the influence of the opium trade has been wholly injurious to our commercial interests in China; and from this point of view no sufficient defence can be set up on its behalf.

But while admitting these facts in the past, those who would defend the continuance of the traffic to-day may perhaps urge that the mischief done is beyond remedy, and that the increased commercial intercourse which might ensue on the adoption of a changed policy on the part of the British Government would not sufficiently compensate for the loss of the Indian revenue which would of course result. On this point it is obvious that an absolutely correct answer is impossible, but it may nevertheless be useful to indicate what may fairly be expected under such changed circumstances. It may first be observed, that the ability of the Chinese to pay £16,800,000 for opium at least implies their power of taking British manufactures to a vastly increased amount if only their expenditure for opium had ceased. Even Commissioner Lin in 1839 used much the same argument. We find him urging in his edict to the foreigners of March 4 in that year, that ' supposing you cut off and cast away your traffic in the ' single article of opium, then the other business which you do ' will be much increased : you will thereon reap your three- ' fold profit comfortably, and you may, as previously, go on ac- ' quiring wealth in abundance.' To similar effect the Governor of Canton, writing to Captain Elliott, Sept. 28, 1837 (China Papers, 1840, p. 239), holds out to him as an inducement to send away the opium receiving-ships that ' thus the source of ' the evil may be closed . . . and the path of commercial inter- ' course may for ever be kept open to all good foreigners.

But that this not only was but still is the feeling of the Chinese Government is evident from the statements made by Sir Rutherford Alcock before the Committee on East India Finance of 1871, when he said (Q. 5728), 'If I had been able 'during the recent revision of the treaty to hold out any 'distinct promise or assurance that as regarded missionaries 'and opium, which are their two great grievances, something 'should be done more or less restrictive that would meet 'their wishes, I believe that I might have got any facilities 'for our trade that I had chosen to demand. My great 'difficulty was that I could offer them nothing in either 'direction.' In the memorial on the Opium Trade presented by Prince Kung to Sir Rutherford Alcock, already quoted, the Chinese ministers remind him that they had on several occasions referred to the opium trade as being prejudicial to the general interest of commerce, an observation which they repeat in the course of the memorial, and they urge the arrangement of a plan for the joint prohibition of the traffic as the one way of causing 'the people to put aside all ill-feeling, 'and so to strengthen their friendly relations as to place them 'for ever beyond fear of disturbance.' This testimony as to the goodwill of the Chinese Government towards a change of policy may be supported by evidence as to the ability to fulfil the expectations which it may have raised. On this point the evidence is not wholly conclusive. On the one side it has been urged that the Chinese are essentially a self-sufficing people, and that they really have very few wants which need the help of Western civilization to supply. At the same time there is some strong evidence on the other side. Dr. Williamson, a well-known traveller and missionary in China, is of opinion (Moule, 'Opium Question,' p. 34) that 'there is a tremendous 'market yet in China for all kinds of foreign wares.' Dr. Dudgeon, the well-known medical missionary at Pekin, declares that, 'were the whole country thrown open to our commerce;

'our manufactures introduced; railways, etc., allowed, and
'the importation of opium forbidden, and it rendered piracy to
'introduce it by all governments, then there would dawn as it
'were a new era on the world and on China. Our merchants,
'and India too, might well afford to give up its [opium's]
'production and transit. The exchange between the different
'countries would soon rearrange itself. The Chinese would
'be saved from beggary, starvation, and death, and they would
'become our best customers. The rich soil of India would
'easily produce the more generous fruits of the earth. A little
'economy wisely exercised among themselves, and a helping
'hand for a few years if necessary from the *then* enriched
'British and Chinese merchants, and the difficulties would
'soon and easily be overcome . . . China cannot take both
'goods and opium, and the question for our merchants
'therefore is, which branch of the industry should be encouraged' ('*Friend of China*,' p. 279). Elsewhere he says,
'Were this traffic abolished there is almost nothing in
'the way of progress, in opening up the country, and in faci-
'litating the trade that they (the Chinese) are not, I believe,
'prepared to do.' Sir Rutherford Alcock has already been
quoted, but he may once more be called upon to conclude
this part of the discussion. Long ago he told his government 'that though China then ranked very low as a market
'for the produce of our looms and manufacturing industry,
'and though its people are poor consumers, yet under other
'auspices and more favourable conditions the Chinese empire
'might within the next twenty years offer a vast field of com-
'mercial activity, and would soon lead to a consumption of
'manufactured goods ten times as large as any at present
'existing.' If the prophecy has not yet been fulfilled, it is
chiefly because the chief conditions have not as yet been
complied with. But it is not too much to hope that when
the 'more favourable conditions' are found in the restric-

tion and abolition of the opium traffic, the long unfulfilled prediction will speedily find a more than ample accomplishment.

It only remains, before closing this chapter of the subject, to add a few words as to its general bearing on our political and international relations with the Chinese people, and the probable advantages of an altered policy. The evil influences of the drug in at least justifying the exclusive and unfriendly attitude of the Chinese government has already been sufficiently dwelt on. At the same time it should not be forgotten that it heavily handicaps England in comparison with the other European nations with whom the Chinese may at any time have dealings, and that in consequence she will not be able to secure easily the good offices or the good-will of the Chinese government should she ever require them. And though such a contingency may be improbable, yet it is by no means impossible, especially when we remember the magnitude and the dispersion of British interests in the Eastern hemisphere. The dangers of Russian aggression on the stability of our Indian empire may no doubt be remote, but, at the same time, it can hardly be advantageous for us that China should ally herself with the Czar, a policy of which there have been some indications. Nor should we forget that the political atmosphere of the East is, equally with the natural, doubtful and uncertain. Storms and disturbances, involving disastrous consequences, may arise in a sky apparently serene, and with but little warning. The magnitude or the complications of such an event cannot of course be predicted, but it would certainly be rash to exclude them from calculation. Hitherto the Chinese have only known us as a conquering people, and as energetic and perhaps not too scrupulous traders, and we can consequently hardly expect them to cherish towards us any feelings of friendship. Would it not be worth while to try the effect of kindness and generosity on that great nation. Though an ancient, almost prehistoric people, they are by no means effete or without influence in their own and other quarters of the globe. And in this connection the Chinese immigrations, which of late years have attracted notice, should not be overlooked. Is it not worth some sacrifice to stand well with a nation that can send forth into the world such an ever-spreading flood of humanity; and to prevent them from spreading hostile feelings towards us in the different nations of the earth?

But apart from all such considerations, there is one, perhaps less obvious, but mightier, more momentous, and more inevitable, which demands our most serious attention—it is the certain, though oft-forgotten, fact that wickedness and wrong-doing are sure sooner or later to bring about their own penalties. For the laws of morality—whether they be called the laws of God or the laws of nature is immaterial—are never to be violated with impunity, and the great truth they inculcate, that what is morally wrong can never be politically right, will certainly find its fulfilment in our case as in every other. And as sure as there is a God that judgeth the world, so surely will our long course of injustice, if not atoned for and repented of, and that speedily, be avenged by some gigantic disaster. If not, we ourselves, at any rate our children, will find by dire experience that the old Roman expressed historic truth as well as poetic feeling in the lines:—

> 'Raro antecedentem scelestum
> Deseruit pede Poena claudo.'

CHAPTER IV.

THE INFLUENCE OF THE TRAFFIC ON CHRISTIAN MISSIONS.

HITHERTO this question has been discussed solely in its relation to the moral and material interests of the English people. It possesses however another, and with some perhaps a more important, side which claims a little attention. While the pre-eminence of England among the nations of the world in political and material advancement is admitted, her high position in Christendom as the representative of the Christian faith can hardly be denied. But if this may be a cause for rejoicing, it is much more a reason for special care and circumspection in all our doings, since the greater our position for good, the greater our responsibility if we fail to act up to it, and the greater our certain condemnation if our conduct brings aught of reproach upon the holy religion we profess. It needs however but a cursory view to discern that our practice of the great principles of our Christian faith is often far short of our professions, and that our conduct both public and private is in too many instances at variance with that teaching by which we profess to be guided. Nor is it too much to say that our national shortcomings in this matter have largely aided the spread of scepticism and infidelity which has been so marked of late years. If, then, we find the shortcomings of professed Christians urged here as an argument against the truth of their religion, must we not expect the same experience abroad? Must not the religion we proclaim be judged among the heathen rather by the deeds of its professors than by the exhortations of its preachers? Must we not expect to find that the nations to whom we offer our faith will estimate its value by the results which they may observe it to produce among ourselves? 'By their 'fruits ye shall know them,' is a maxim as obvious to the heathen as to the Christian.

How, then, do these considerations bear upon our relations with China and the efforts of our missionaries to spread the truth of the Gospel in that vast empire? It has already been shown that one principal feature of our relations with China is our connection with the traffic in opium, a traffic which at least is not beneficial to the Chinese, and not carried on with their full consent or approbation. Moreover, we have ourselves officially informed them that our 'religion induces to 'the practice of virtue, and teaches men to do as they would 'be done by.' Consequently the inconsistency of our national conduct and our national profession is too obvious to be overlooked by the most careless observer. The Chinese however are both too shrewd and too acute not to draw the natural conclusion as to the value of the religion which we would fain teach them. When they see that the Christian religion produces such effects among Englishmen, can we expect them to believe that in their own case its results will be different? And that this is no imaginary argument is shown by the most ample testimony. Missionaries on all sides give the same witness. Dr. Medhurst tells us:—' Almost 'the first word uttered by a Chinese when anything is said 'concerning the excellence of Christianity is, Why do Chris- 'tians bring us opium, and bring it directly in defiance of 'our laws? The vile drug has destroyed my son, has ruined 'my brother, and well-nigh led me to beggar my wife and 'children. Surely those who import such a deleterious sub- 'stance, and injure me for the sake of gain, cannot be in 'possession of a better religion than my own.' The Bishop of Hong Kong says: 'If those who profess to doubt the 'magnitude of this obstacle to the progress of Christianity 'could hear the more patriotic of the Chinese, frequently 'with a sarcastic smile, ask the missionaries if they were con-'nected with those who brought them poison, which so many 'of their countrymen ate and perished, they would perceive 'that it is vain—I will not say vain—but it is certainly in-'consistent in us as a nation to send the Bible to China.' Sixteen missionaries working in China and belonging to different nations and denominations, in the spring of 1875 stated: 'The fact that people of Christian nations engage in 'the traffic, and especially that Great Britain supplies the 'China market with opium, is constantly urged as a plausible 'and patent objection to Christianity.'—(Sir E. Fry, 'England, ' China, and Opium,' p. 23.)

But further, as a matter of mere experience, it may be urged that the influence of the opium trade in increasing the exclusiveness and objection to foreign intercourse so characteristic of the Chinese which has been already noticed, must in so far have been a hindrance to the spread of missionary efforts. For it is obvious that free intercourse with the people and facilities for ready communication are especially necessary for the propagation of a new faith. It is clearly impossible for a preacher, however earnest and eloquent he may be, to convince his hearers if he is regarded by them as the representative of unjust dealings or an unfriendly purpose. If however it be urged that the exclusive and hostile attitude of the Chinese is natural to them, and independent of the influence of the opium traffic, it may again be remarked, that our conduct in this matter justified the treatment received, while a different course of action could hardly have failed in time to produce better effects. If, moreover, against all this be set the ' opening up' of China to Christian missions, which has been one result of our wars with China and our conflicts with her people, it is much to be feared that the set-off must be wholly disallowed. The manifest injustice of these wars in their conception and their execution has already been pointed out, and can hardly be controverted; and any attempt to maintain that the Gospel of peace can in any way be advanced by conduct in direct contradiction to its most sacred truths, must inevitably fail. Even if the results had been less unfavourable, it would always have remained true that the surest and quickest way of introducing our faith to the hearts of a foreign people is to base our dealings on the grand principles it teaches, and to show in our actions and deeds the superiority of the new doctrines that we desire to propagate.

But there are other considerations of special force with reference to the spread of Christianity in China. It is, as we all know, ' no mere system of abstract philosophy, no mere ' code of ethical precepts;' it claims to be the working energising principle that should actuate and inform all the deeds of its adherents, and cause them to shape their lives and conduct after the example and pattern it presents. If then the heathen or the unbeliever finds in the professors of this exalted and ideal faith marked shortcomings and conspicuous deficiencies in the fulfilment of its precepts, they cannot but infer the weakness and impotence of such an ineffectual creed. What wonder if they should bid its apostles first to enforce its principles on its professed disciples before they attempt to gain proselytes elsewhere. May they not well argue that a religion which makes such claims and permits such deficiencies must be based upon some fallacy, and that at any rate it is not one for which they are prepared to surrender their traditional beliefs?

But this matter has a special importance for English Christians. The connection of their country with the opium trade places its missionaries in an exceptionally invidious and disadvantageous position. The missionaries of other nations can, when pressed with the opium trade, say they are free from the stain, that their hands are clean, that they cannot be brought under the same condemnation. Thus it results that English missionaries become more and more identified in the minds of the Chinese people with the opium traffic, so dishonouring to Christianity and so injurious to man, a connection which must inevitably hinder their efforts in the cause, and make the results of their work much less satisfactory than it might be under more favourable circumstances. But can the English people expect a blessing on their efforts in this direction as long as they allow this great evil to go on unchecked? May it not well be the case 'that our national sin 'in this matter has separated us from our God and turned 'aside the reward that he would otherwise have bestowed 'upon our labours. Have we not rather deserved to hear the 'terrible rebuke, ' When ye spread forth your hands I will hide 'mine eyes from you : yea, when ye make many prayers I 'will not hear: your hands are full of blood: wash you, make 'you clean: put away the evil of your doings before mine 'eyes; cease to do evil; learn to do well'?

If then in all these ways there is good reason to think that the opium traffic increases the difficulties—which must always be great—of missionary enterprise in China, does it not furnish a powerful argument for all who profess and call themselves Christians, to use every effort for the removal of this moral stigma on our nation, for the termination of our national connection with this enormous wickedness? The moral effects of such a policy on the Chinese would certainly be most favourable to the cause of Christian Missions. Then indeed the Gospel of Christ would appear more worthy of its name, more consistent with its fundamental principles, and therefore more deserving the respectful attention and the acceptance of the Chinese people. The spread of the truth among the inhabitants of that vast empire would be freer and less hampered; the strong prejudices which have hitherto made it suspected and have brought it into hatred and contempt would cease to be felt; and Christianity would be able to win its way into the hearts of the Chinese people. Then, all its inherent forces, its active energies for doing good, its power to suffer all things if only it may win souls, instead of being stifled in their birth, would have free scope and would certainly prevail. Thus indeed will the religion of Jesus at last 'open China to Europe and interpret Europe to China,' and will usher in a new era in the history of Christian missions. Then a mighty impulse shall be given to the work of evangelisation in all the distant provinces, and the word of the Lord shall increase and multiply among the kingdoms of the east:—

'Then shall our land send forth her sons and daughters,
'Baal shall bow down before the Spirit's sword,
'And as the sea sounds with her sounding waters,
'So shall Cathay with the Knowledge of the Lord.'

CHAPTER V.

CONCLUSION.

THE general conclusions to which our investigations have brought us may now be briefly stated thus. On moral grounds we are compelled to admit that it obviously and undeniably conflicts with the first principles of morality; and also that, though extenuations were urged in mitigation of this verdict, it has appeared that while these palliatory pleas could claim in some cases a certain plausibility, they yet failed to satisfy the test of a rigorous and careful scrutiny. Thus the contention that the effects of opium-smoking were not harmful was shown to be the case in exceptions rather than the rule: the alleged insincerity of the Chinese proved on investigation to be due, partly to administrative impotence, partly and chiefly to violent action on our part and our practical encouragement of the unlawful trade. When tested by the touchstone of political expediency the arguments on each side were somewhat more equalised, virtually resolving themselves into the question whether India was to continue to receive larger additions to her revenue, practically by the restriction on British commerce and manufactures, a conflict in which the balance of probabilities at least was against the further continuance of the traffic. Further, the question of its influence on Christian missions was shortly considered, and proved to be in the highest degree injurious and harmful to the spread of Christianity.

If then the verdict on all points of the indictment be adverse, there is no need for hesitation in pointing out the course which alone England can adopt. She must determine to shake off without unnecessary delay the grievous responsibility under which she now labours, she must withdraw from her connection with a traffic that merits such unqualified condemnation. But if this be admitted, the question still remains as to the best and most effectual method by which the policy of abandonment can be carried out. And in this connection it should be remarked that the restriction and ultimate prohibition of the opium cultivation in Bengal must be a main feature in the new departure. For merely to withdraw the government monopoly, and thus to leave the field free for the advent of countless individual manufacturers, would only, in Lord Hartington's words, effect 'the demoralisation of our 'own subjects,' in addition to inflicting added injury to the Chinese people. As under the present regime the cultivation of the poppy is prohibited in 95 per cent. of the country, there would seem to be no insuperable obstacle to preventing its cultivation in the remaining 5 per cent.: more especially as the poppy is a plant very easily detected, and the manufacture of the drug not a process that can be carried on in secret.

Another point of capital importance would be to obtain the concurrence of the Chinese government in a similar restrictive policy in the provinces of the Celestial Empire. It has indeed been asserted by the Indian government that the power of the Chinese to carry out such regulations is absent, and certainly it has been very rarely if ever exercised hitherto: at the same time the experiment is worth trying whether or not the co-operation instead of the antagonism of England would enable China successfully to enforce such ordinances. For the first few years it might perhaps be unadvisable to prohibit the entire importation, but restrictive regulations, enforced by the English and Chinese authorities in concert, could hardly fail to produce considerable constraint. Thus the way would be paved for the speedy withdrawal of the entire trade better than if it were precipitately terminated, a course of action which would undoubtedly cause numerous difficulties and no small amount of irritation both in India and China.

But, subject to this one qualification, the need for action in the matter is immediate and urgent, for in a few years the evil may, we are told, be beyond the power of man to eradicate or to cure, and thus England, if she delays, will have lost a grand opportunity for rectifying her relations between China and its people, and of putting herself before them in a more favourable light.

The financial question, as to how the deficiency in the Indian budget which would probably result can be replaced, it is not necessary to discuss further than it has been discussed already. For if the gradual withdrawal which has just been suggested be carried out judiciously it is more than possible that time would be allowed for discovering the requisite means, and that expedients might present themselves in proportion as the necessity for them became apparent. Moreover it has been admitted, that if Indian resources were inadequate to the emergency the assistance of England must be forthcoming to supply the deficiency, and must provide for the necessary expenses which the recognition of international morality might demand from her. Nor can there be much doubt that when the facts and character of the opium traffic become more widely known, the moral sense of the people will willingly respond to the demand, and authorise its representatives in Parliament not to refuse assent, even though the sum might involve some millions of extra taxation.

And when that eventful, but it is hoped not too far distant, day shall dawn, and when a British Minister rising in his place in Parliament shall announce to the assembled Commons the adoption by the Government of a new and more righteous

policy in this matter, and shall propose the necessary vote of credit—not for the expenses of some projected warfare, but for the establishment of love, peace, and international goodwill—' when a British Minister shall speak so, and a British
' public shall applaud him speaking, then shall the nation be
' so glorious that her praise, instead of exploding from within,
' from loud civic mouths, shall come to her from without, as
' all worthy praise must, from the alliances she has fostered,
' and from the populations she has saved.'

www.ingramcontent.com/pod-product-compliance
Lightning Source LLC
Chambersburg PA
CBHW020158170426
43199CB00010B/1096